O'Reagan's

by
Allen Price

New Harbor Press
RAPID CITY, SD

Copyright © 2024 by Allen Price.

All rights reserved. No part of this publication may be reproduced, distributed or transmitted in any form or by any means, including photocopying, recording, or other electronic or mechanical methods, without the prior written permission of the publisher, except in the case of brief quotations embodied in critical reviews and certain other noncommercial uses permitted by copyright law. For permission requests, write to the publisher, addressed "Attention: Permissions Coordinator," at the address below.

Price/New Harbor Press
1601 Mt Rushmore Rd, Ste 3288
Rapid City, SD 57701
www.NewHarborPress.com

O'Reagan's/Allen Price. -- 1st ed.
ISBN 978-1-63357-299-7

To my wife and children who supported me every step of the way, eager for me to read to them what I wrote each day as a bedtime story, well, until it got too scary for them.

PROLOGUE

IT HAD BEEN a long week. Special Agent-In-Charge Karena Garcia had been in this crappy little Maine town far too long. One day would be too long. July 2014 was hotter and stickier than normal, with daily highs topping one hundred degrees. And the mosquitoes and blackflies were so thick you had to wear long pants and long sleeves. Even Muskol, the bug spray with the highest DEET content she could find, didn't help much (but God love the person who went into the deep woods of Baxter State Park without it!) By the time she got back to her room after her eighth day of searching, she had hundreds of puffy, itchy bites. For the life of her she couldn't figure out how. She had covered herself head to toe and even taped her pant legs tight around her ankles. Still, every day, more bites. Were mosquitoes biting her through her clothes?

She tossed back two antihistamines and slipped into a cool shower, eager to wash the sweat, dirt, and bug spray from her skin and hair. Earlier she had slipped in the mud and fallen into a swampy mess. Disgusting. Why in the hell was she even out here? She had better things to do than tramp around in the wilderness looking for a couple of lost teenagers — ok, twenty-somethings. The local forest service should be handling this, not the FBI.

But one call to her boss from Congressman Peter Benson of Tennessee, and here she was. Mr. Benson had been calling all his contacts in government, claiming his son and two friends had met some violent fate. Since he had a long list of enemies and had received many threats against his life and those of his family members, his call to the FBI was answered and action taken. More of a cover-your-ass move than one of real concern.

Benson was one of those politicians who somehow got elected despite his big mouth. More obnoxious and sleazy than Donald Trump, Benson aligned his policies with anyone willing to line his pockets — though there was never any proof of wrongdoing, despite all the accusations. He must have dirt on everyone on Capitol Hill given how much support he seemed to have. He was slime, as far as Karena was concerned, and didn't deserve the special attention. But she had her orders. "Get your ass to Maine, take a half dozen agents, coordinate with the local sheriff, state police, and Fish and Game. Find those kids!" her boss had yelled when she'd protested.

When she arrived, she met her state police liaison, Alice Maxwell, in Millinocket. Alice was her kind of cop — strong, smart, and intuitive. The kind of cop she could partner with. The two of them had quickly established a bond and were determined to figure out what was going on in the woods around this sleepy little town.

According to Alice, this wasn't the first time people had gone missing out here. This was just the first time someone important enough had forced a real investigation. So far, Alice knew of nine missing people in the last four years. All of them within one week of the local music festival. There was a pattern here that no one wanted to notice. The other disappearances had been given minimal manpower and minimal time, the missing written off as lost in the woods after short searches by Fish and Game. The local sheriff, Alex Johnson, didn't seem to take it seriously, and Alice couldn't get any support from her superiors to complete a thorough investigation. The only response had been a few posters stating that venturing off into the woods was dangerous.

So, here Karena was, eight days into a search of the forest, coordinating with Fish and Game and state police, and all they had to show for their efforts was a couple of encounters with wildlife — two moose, a black bear, a few deer, and what one agent swore was a mountain lion. The team was exhausted.

To make matters worse, Sheriff Johnson insisted that he be the one to interview the locals. Any request to speak to them herself, and Karena was shut down immediately. He was the sheriff, and she needed to play nice. Johnson claimed he had questioned everyone in town. He said a few local business owners remembered seeing the young men, but that was all. The kids had been in all three pubs and the supermarket. The security camera on the bank's ATM showed each of them making withdrawals during the music festival. Their tents were still set up and untouched (as far as anyone could tell) in the field at the Ramirez farm. And that was it. Nothing else. The boys' blue Toyota FJ Cruiser sat at the edge of the field near their campsite. There was nothing of consequence inside the vehicle, just a bunch of fast-food receipts and garbage from their trip to the festival.

Despite exhausting all efforts, including air support, K-9 teams, and local search teams, they had nothing. The dogs hadn't even picked up their scent, which Karena thought was strange, as it hadn't rained since well before they went missing.

Karena had a suspicion, deep in her gut, that there was more to this story than met the eye. She had no real reason to feel this way, but she knew she was missing something. Perhaps it was just the fact that three young people had gone missing without a trace. Or it could be the weird way some of the townspeople looked at her. Maybe it was how they appeared helpful, but said nothing that actually helped. She had an uneasy feeling that they were hiding something, and Alice agreed with her. But they had no proof.

Sheriff Johnson had already moved on from the case when Karena arrived. He'd simply put them down as missing persons, lost in the woods. "I see it all the time," he told her. "Thousands of people come to the festival and go for walks in the woods. Sometimes we find them, sometimes we don't. We lose a couple almost every year. I don't have the manpower for so many exhaustive searches. I do my best, but there are miles and miles of wilderness out there."

No one had seen the boys head into the woods. Yet there was no sign of them, anywhere, other than their camp site. They hadn't bought any hiking gear, nor had they brought any with them. They were from the city; perhaps they'd overestimated their abilities and were oblivious to the dangers.

Karena's call back to DC wasn't going to be pleasant. Her recommendation: end the search and list the three young men as missing. There was really nothing more they could do — at least not officially. Alice had promised to keep poking around and to call her if anything turned up.

With no evidence to keep her in Harrington any longer, she hoped to be back in her own bed by tomorrow. Why anyone would want to live in this bug-infested hell hole, thirty-five miles from the nearest real town, was beyond her.

But what was she missing?

CHAPTER 1

"ELIZABETH," MOM CALLED from the kitchen. "You'd better grab some breakfast before you leave." Mom never would call me Beth. "Elizabeth is your name," she'd say. "If I wanted to call you Beth, I would have named you Beth."

I'd been looking forward to today for months, and I had forgotten to eat this morning as I got ready. My friends and I had long talked about heading to the 2019 Mainestock Music Festival in Harrington, Maine, just west of Millinocket, nestled inside Baxter State Park. I had just finished up veterinary school in PEI and was set to start my new job at Douglas Animal Hospital in a few weeks. This might be the last time the gang could take a trip like this, now that we were all adulting. Working for a living would definitely be a big change.

I was very excited about starting at the clinic. It was the largest in the Fredericton area. During my internship there, I'd had the chance to go out to some area farms and assist with the large animals. Mostly I was giving needles and patching up small wounds, but I did get to help deliver a calf that was breach. And we had one exciting call, when a calf got attacked by a coyote. The mom fought her off, but the little guy sustained some nasty cuts, so we nursed her back to health for a few days.

I'd wanted to be a vet since I was kid. Ever since the time a robin flew into our living room window. I took it in, laid it in a box, and talked to it for hours. I even dug up some worms and fed it like a momma bird would feed her young — except for the chewing it first and regurgitating it, that is! After a few hours, Dad and I took it outside, and it flew to the nearest branch of the maple tree in our front yard. It looked back at me as if to say "thanks," sang a little song, and then flew off. It was then and there that I decided to be a vet, and now I was finally realizing my dream.

I'd been to Baxter State Park before with my church youth group. The last time, two years ago, we had camped at the foot of Mount Katahdin at Roaring Brook Campground and hiked up the Chimney Pond Trail in the backcountry.

We left camp just before dawn as we wanted to do the round trip to the summit in one day. We stopped for lunch at the Chimney Pond Campground, where we lit a small fire and cooked a few hot dogs. The scenery and the lake were beautiful! I couldn't imagine a more breathtaking setting. The lake was smooth as glass except for the trail of a loon, swimming across it and occasionally dropping under the water only to reappear a moment later, farther away. I could almost see myself and my future husband building a little cabin in the woods and spending our lives fishing and swimming and hiking together in this pristine wilderness, away from the stresses of city life.

After our lunch break, we took Cathedral Trail up to the top. We all yelled, "Top of the world, Ma!" when we reached the summit. One of the leaders had brought along some non-alcoholic sparkling cider. She popped the cork, and we all lifted a glass to our climb, to God, and to Canada, as if we had just conquered America like some explorers of old.

Most of the group went back down Cathedral Trail, as it was the easier course and several of them were scared of heights. I and a handful of others ventured down the other way, across the Knife Edge with its breathtaking views (and scary drops!). At one point I almost lost my balance and thought I was going to take a plunge down the cliffside. I pictured bouncing off the one-hundred-foot ledge below, only to free-fall several hundred more feet to my death. Then a hand reached out to steady me. I've never been so glad to have a church leader close by! After I caught my breath, I looked out at the vast wilderness around me. I could see lakes, rivers and streams, and way off in the distance, I swore I could see Millinocket itself. An eagle screeched and another answered. It was the most awe-inspiring scenery I had ever seen. I almost forgot my near-death experience. Almost. I took in a deep breath of the cool, fresh air and thought to myself, "I need to get back here one day." It was the most invigorated I've ever felt.

After we crossed The Knife Edge, we went on to Pamola Peak. It wasn't quite as high, but the view was equally amazing. The forest below was shimmering from the glimmer of the sun playing off the many ponds, lakes, and streams. From there it was down Dudley Trail to Chimney Pond, where we met the rest of the group.

The guys dared us to take a swim in the clear, icy waters. A few of my friends jumped right in and splashed away.

Others made their way in more slowly. I finally decided to join them. It was chilly in the mountains, but after such a long hike I was hot and sweaty, and cleaning up would feel great. Besides, I didn't want the boys to have all the fun — or the bragging rights!

I couldn't have anticipated the icy cold. It took my breath away as I jumped in. Goosebumps rose on my skin almost immediately and my hair stood up on end. I couldn't turn back, so I dove under, almost breathing in a lung full of water as my body reacted to the cold. When I popped out of the water, gasping, the guys were all cheering.

Eventually, we all headed back down the Chimney Pond Trail to our campground. We made a bonfire, cooked dinner, and ate S'mores for dessert. Someone had brought a guitar, and we sang some campfire songs, told stories, and enjoyed each other's company until the wee hours of the morning.

We woke to the sound of our leaders making pancakes over an open fire, along with bacon and eggs. We had a short Bible study (it was Sunday after all), and then we headed home. I don't know about the rest of the group, but I slept almost the whole way. I was exhausted but happy.

Now, with school behind me, I couldn't wait to go back. If the rest of the park was half as beautiful as Mount Katahdin, our trip would be awesome. Even with Jason and Anna now glued at the hip. Anna had been my best friend since grade school, and Jason was my ex. I was still angry that she was dating him. Especially after what he did. She didn't know the whole story, so I couldn't blame her, but our relationship wasn't the same.

CHAPTER 2

THE CAR RIDE would take about four hours. The first two and half would take us into Millinocket, another hour would get us to Harrington, inside Baxter State Park, and an additional half hour would be for getting across the border (and taking pee breaks, of course).

We left for the festival a day early, on Monday, in hopes of avoiding the long line at the border crossing between Woodstock, New Brunswick and Houlton, Maine. It was the most popular crossing to get to Baxter State Park as it was an hour faster than crossing from St. Stephen into Calais. Our plan was to arrive mid-afternoon, set up camp, and scope out the town. The one-hour time difference in our favour on the way there should make it easy. That is, if CBP (Customs and Border Protection) was in a good mood. We'd heard that since the legalization of marijuana by the Canadian Government, CBP was more vigilant than ever, especially with younger people. Fingers crossed!

I was the last to be picked up — at "9:30 sharp!" Jason had said. I was the only single person on the trip (sigh). I hadn't really dated since Jason and I broke up in the summer of 2013, after grade twelve. After Jason hurt me, I was having trouble trusting guys. We'd started dating in grade nine — puppy love, our parents called it. We continued to date all through high school and were quite serious by the end of it. We even talked about getting married. In the Fredericton High School Yearbook — Go Black Cats! — we were voted most likely to stay together. We were third place for the King and Queen of prom. (You guessed it, Peter LaFrance and Megan Wishart — the star centre for the hockey team and his cheerleader girlfriend — were named King and Queen. Talk about your stereotype.)

When prom ended, a bunch of us went for dinner at The Diplomat, a 24-hour restaurant in town. There was me and Jason, Anna and her boyfriend Steve (whatever happened to him?), Jill and Ben, and a few others I can't remember. What I didn't know was that Jason had reserved a room at the Delta Hotel next door for us. He only told me after we had eaten a delicious Chinese Combo Plate and were getting ready to leave. He was so nervous. I think he thought I was going to say no, but I didn't. I'd been hoping he would do something like this. I had dreamed of being with him. He was so gentle when we were together, and thoughtful and kind. My heart skipped a beat if I even spotted his car driving down the street. And it didn't hurt that he had a great body. Not too muscular, but I could make out each and every ab on his midsection — and those arms and that chest!

In the end, he was even more nervous than me, I think. We made some idle chitchat about who danced with whom, made fun of whoever was were there alone, and talked a little about the future. It was just a bunch of nothing as we waited for each other to make the first move. Can you say *awkward*?

Then we kissed. This kiss was different, as we were so filled with anticipation. It was actually better! I felt myself become aroused like never before. We'd never done this. We'd come close once or twice but never moved beyond some groping and taking off our shirts. Prom night was meant to be different. We kissed for a while, and then he started by taking off my shirt.

In the following days, I felt we were drawing even closer. That is, until my period was late. I told him right away, and he immediately bolted. And when I say bolted, I mean he literally left town. Gone. No email. No phone call. Nothing. When I talked to his parents, they said he went to Toronto to visit his cousins. It seemed like they knew. I couldn't believe he was able to leave so fast. I couldn't believe he *would* leave that fast. I thought I knew him better than that. I guess he was just like all the other guys out there. He acted like a total ass.

When I did get my period ten days late, I was so relieved. But by then I knew he wasn't the man I thought he was. When he came back to town three weeks later, he reached out and tried to apologize, but I wouldn't listen. I never told my parents the whole story, only that he had been a jerk, and we were done. They supported me without too many questions. I think they assumed he'd tried something, and left me when I said no. If they only knew. My older sister Jodi was a little more persistent, but even she gave up after a few days. Jodi was away at McGill University studying to be a doctor, so she was always busy studying, or working at the Dr. Everett Chalmers Hospital during her time home.

I never actually told anyone what happened. Not even Anna. She knew I was hurting, and that Jason was the cause, but that was it. She came by the house a little more often. Called more often. She even forced me to go out with her to eat and see a movie. I was a miserable friend for far too long, but Anna stayed true and tolerated my up and down moods. Eventually I got through it. I wouldn't say I got over Jason, but I got through it.

And then, Jason and Anna got together. I think he assumed that she knew everything and was dating him anyway. How could I tell her now? She was so happy with him. She called me when he asked her out six months ago, just to make sure I wouldn't be mad. It hurt that she would even ask, but I chose to be the bigger person. I would rise above it with my head held high. We hadn't been as close since they started dating, but I was trying. I did, after all, tell her it was ok.

I popped out of the shower at just after nine, ready to set off on our musical adventure. I took care as I dried off my right ankle. I had recently gotten a small tattoo, a cross, and it was still a little tender.

Of course, they were early. I had finished getting dressed and was drying my hair when I heard the car horn. It was only 9:15! Jodi called up to me that they were here, like I couldn't hear the horn. I turned off the hair dryer, picked up my bag, and bounced down the stairs. I paused halfway down to look at a picture. It was Mom and Dad on their wedding day. I couldn't get over how much I looked like her at that age. Same strawberry-blonde hair. Same blue eyes. Same freckles across the tops of our cheeks and noses. We were the same height at five feet, eight inches, and we both had the same figure. I bet we weighed the same, too — 130 pounds of athletic beauty!

I was wearing a pair of shorts and a tank top. Perfect for a car trip in the hot weather. I snagged a Fuji apple off the counter (my favourite), gave my mom a kiss and told her to kiss Dad for me (he was at work), yelled a goodbye to Jodi, and then I was out the door. I tossed my bag in the trunk of Jason's Honda Pilot and went back to the garage for my camping gear. When everything was loaded, I took my place alone in the third row. Being single had its advantages.

Jason and Anna were up front, with Dwayne and Tia snuggled in the second row. Off we went, through town and up to the Trans-Canada Highway. Soon we would be at the border, and then on to the Mainestock Music Festival. I couldn't wait to see all the bands, but especially Ed Sheeran. It was rumoured that Ed and Taylor Swift were going to perform together again at the festival. I loved their song *Everything Has Changed* from a few years earlier. Other headliners were Billie Eilish, Ariana Grande, and Bruno Mars, one each night from Wednesday to Sunday. There was even some Canadian talent, like Justin Bieber and Drake. Music would start on Wednesday at seven p.m. and then go from two p.m. until midnight all the other days.

I had never been to such a big concert event before. Tickets weren't cheap at $400 American, but I was sure it would be worth it. I planned to buy a concert T-shirt or two, and who knew what else. I also hoped to do a little hiking. I had brought along a collapsible pole in hopes of catching some fish for breakfast or dinner for everyone. I had read that the rivers and lakes were filled with trout and landlocked salmon.

CHAPTER 3

WE MADE OUR first stop in Woodstock, just before the border crossing. The girls all had to pee. So did the boys, but they said they only went because we were already stopped. I laughed at the sign outside the restrooms: Boys to the Left 'Cause Girls Are Always Right. I punched Dwayne in the arm and said, "Don't you forget it!" Tia giggled.

The last fifteen minutes to the border was filled with talk between the couples while I sat in the back, silently listening. Jason and Anna were laughing about their dinner date the night before. Apparently, the server had spilled a whole tray of drinks on Jason when she slipped on some ice dropped by the busboy. I smiled at the thought, wishing I had seen it. A small part of me wished it had been hot coffee, something to cause a little pain.

Tia talked to Dwayne about her job. Tia worked at Chapters as the manager in charge of bargain books and new releases. She had just been acknowledged for her leadership, as their store's percentage of bargain book sales was the highest in the country for the year. It came with a two-hundred-and-fifty-dollar bonus and two paid days off. They were coming up with ideas for how to spend the money on a little trip for two. We arrived at the border before they figured it out. I leaned in and said, "Tia, that's terrific! Congratulations."

We all got our passports ready and gave them to Jason, who was driving, and rolled down all the windows. My father had suggested this: "And ensure no one is wearing sunglasses. That way Customs will see you have nothing to hide. Sometimes a car of young people going through the border will get harsh treatment. Just be cool and do what you're asked." Boy, was he right.

Jason handed the passports to the CBP agent, who took what felt like an eternity to enter them into the computer. Then he didn't hand them back, but stepped out of the hut and approached Jason's window.

"Where are you going?" he asked.

"We're headed to the Mainestock Festival in Harrington," Jason replied. This was followed by the usual questions: "Are you all Canadian Citizens? Are you bringing in any firearms? Tobacco? Alcohol? Are you planning on leaving anything behind?" And Jason gave short, honest answers.

He asked us to pull over under the awning and come into the main building. Jason must have rolled his eyes or sighed or something. The agent's attitude turned on a dime.

"Am I inconveniencing you, young man? Are you hiding something? You do realize I can simply turn you around and deny you entry to the United States." To each of these Jason responded with a "No sir" or "Yes sir," but it didn't help. The agent followed us to a parking space and ordered us out of the vehicle. He took the keys from Jason and sent us into the main building.

We went in and were told to take a seat and wait. I got up and asked for the restroom and was pointed to a door at the back. There was no cute sign like in the gas station. An hour in, Dwayne went to the vending machines in the corner and bought each of us a bottle of water.

After two hours, the agent came through the door. We all stood, and with one look from him, sat back down. By now I was fuming. I couldn't believe we were being treated like criminals for trying to go to a concert. Tickets alone had each cost four hundred dollars, and we were going to add hundreds more to the local economy after gas, food, camping, and anything else we bought.

Another forty-five minutes later Agent Asshole called Jason to the counter. When Anna tried to join him, she was turned back. I couldn't hear them, but the agent seemed to have a lot to say. To Jason's credit, he kept his cool. I don't know if I could have. I would probably have been thrown in jail. Jason returned. We could finally leave.

I brought up the rear and almost ran into Dwayne when everyone in front of me stopped short. There, under the awning, was Jason's Pilot. All the doors were open. All the contents, including the spare tire (now flat), jack, tire iron, and floor mats, were on the ground. I opened my mouth to say something and then shut it, realizing just in time that Agent Asshole was right behind me. He had a big grin on his face and said, "Sorry folks, we search, but we don't have to put it all back." And then he walked away.

After our shock wore off, and our anger subsided — a little — we put the Pilot back together. I prayed we didn't get a flat tire on the rest of the drive. Jason must have still been upset because we hadn't been driving twenty minutes when he suddenly slowed down. I looked out the back window. There was a police car behind us, flashing its lights.

Jason showed his driver's license, registration, and insurance when the officer came to his window. She went back to her car, and I watched as she punched the details into her computer. No one said a single word. There was no need.

When the officer returned, she asked Jason where he was going in such a hurry. He started to cry in frustration. In a flood of emotion, he told her the whole story about the border crossing and the ridiculous and baseless search of our vehicle. He told her about how the agent had rubbed it in and then left everything on the ground. He apologized for speeding and said that he hadn't even realized he was doing it. He was just trying not to explode, and could she please just hurry up and give him the ticket so we could get to Millinocket.

As Jason told his story I could see the officer's face soften. Her body language changed, and she relaxed. Then she said, "Well, sir, it sounds like you've had one hell of a day. I'm sorry this was your welcome to the great state of Maine. Please know that not everyone you meet will treat you like the border agent. I'll tell you what, if you promise to slow down, I'll just give you a warning. Now go on your way, and please enjoy the concert. Here's my card, I'm officer Alice Maxwell. If any more trouble should find you, please call me." And that was it. She slapped the top of the Pilot, got back in her patrol car, and drove off.

I said, "Man, Jason, you need to cry more often!" He threw a dirty napkin at me, but I was too far away. Like I said, the third row has its advantages!

The rest of the trip down was uneventful. The car was quiet as we all continued to stew about the border agent and appreciate Officer Alice at the same time.

When we got into Millinocket, it was almost four p.m. Maine time. Even with the hour time difference, we were running late. Thank goodness it wouldn't get dark until eight o'clock.

While the guys took enough stuff out of the back to get at the spare tire and blow it back up, Anna, Tia, and I went into the store and bought cold drinks and ice. When we came out, Jason was gassing up the Pilot while Dwayne was putting the tire back in. I filled the coolers with the ice and helped load the remaining gear.

As we neared the festival grounds, we began to get excited. Our anger and frustration gave way to chat about which artist we were most excited to see. For me it was Ed Sheeran; for Anna, Billie Eilish, and Dwayne said it was Drake for him. Tia said Taylor Swift, and Jason agreed, teasing: "Because she's hot!" Which earned him a hard punch in the shoulder from Anna and lots of laughter from the rest of us.

I noticed that many of the hotels sported signs welcoming concert goers. Most of them had "No Vacancy" lit up and the few that didn't were what I would call seedy motels. It was easy to see that Millinocket benefitted greatly from the festival. Already the streets were full, and restaurants looked busy. By the time the festival began, fifty thousand visitors would flood Harrington, Millinocket, and all the towns within an hour's drive.

We left the gas station and headed towards Harrington. We drove through town and then turned onto Golden Road. As we entered Baxter State Park, we were instantly awed by the dense forest. In the distance I could see Mt. Katahdin and had a rush of great memories from my past trip. We passed a number of lakes and campgrounds. I saw a fish jump in one of the ponds, and I wondered what kind of fish it was. I hoped my folding fishing rod was strong enough to land a big one, or at least some medium sized ones, in one of the lakes or streams.

When we passed Big Eddy Campground, we turned right onto Telos Rd. We crossed Duck Brook and then Telos Road turned into Main Street. Seventy-five minutes after leaving Millinocket, we arrived in Harrington.

The town was already bustling with people. Given the late hour, we decided to go straight to the farm to set up camp and then return to town for dinner. We followed the signs to the farm, turning right and driving through town. Main Street widened at the centre of town and split into two separate lanes divided by with a nice fountain and park in between. I noted a small supermarket, a bank, a town hall, and the sheriff's station among the buildings. As we got to the edge of town, I noted an old house attached to an even older church, both large and foreboding, even in the light. O'Reagan's Funeral Parlour, the sign read. Then we turned right again and saw the farm.

CHAPTER 4

WE PULLED UP to a makeshift gate made of straw bales and a piece of metal fencing, its post stuck into the crack between the bales. There was a crude hut off to the side where a young woman sat shaded from the late afternoon sun.

She came to greet us, introducing herself as Bel, which I assumed was short for Isobel but didn't ask. She was beautiful, with dark brown hair and brown eyes, and was quite tall and slender. Dwayne and Jason also noticed how pretty she was. They smiled and watched her as she walked towards the car.

Bel asked us our names and looked up our reservation on the list on her clipboard. She told us there was a strict quiet time from two a.m. to seven a.m., "So that everyone can get at least a little sleep." During that time, we were not permitted to play music, games, or make any other noise. We didn't think that would be an issue, especially tonight, as we were exhausted from the ordeal of our trip.

We got directions to our campsite, near the back corner, away from the road as we had requested. Bel let us know that there would be shuttle busses moving back and forth from the concert grounds beginning two hours before the first concert of the day and ending 90 minutes after the end of the last. We also learned that, yes, the trailers scattered around the field were indeed shower units. She warned us that the water would be cool as the only heat came from the sun hitting the black hoses on the roof of each trailer. The water itself came from a small creek running along the edge of the property. It was filtered but not suitable for drinking. Potable water was our responsibility.

Bel's father, Carlos, ran the farm. We learned that they grew all manner of vegetables and that he sold much of his crop to the local supermarket. He also had a lot of fruit trees on the property. He had a small apple orchard, that was open in the fall as a U-pick for the townsfolk, along with. pear, plum, and cherry trees. The family even raised a few head of cattle for beef and milk and had a couple of pigs and chickens. They were basically subsistence farmers and sold any extra meat and eggs along with the vegetables, and made their own butter and cheese. I was really excited about the thought of seeing some of the work around the farm. I also thought I'd like to get to know Bel. She was young, maybe eighteen, but seemed so genuine.

I asked her about fishing, and she said Harrington Lake, named after the town, was full of rainbow trout and land-locked salmon. There were also a few bass. She promised to drop by the campsite in the morning and show me a couple of good spots for fishing from shore as well as the two beaches that made for some great swimming. I asked her about Soper Brook, and she said there was some good fishing there as well, but the fish weren't as big as the ones I would catch in the lake. I hoped they tasted as good as I was imagining.

We drove out to the makeshift parking lot Bel had shown us on the site map she provided, and began trekking our gear the three hundred metres from the car to our campsite. I didn't know how we were going to find our way in the dark, especially when the campground was full. We would need to figure something out.

We set up our tents. Our space was painted with orange lines and a site number on the ground. We were number 1128 of 1200. Dwayne and Tia set up their tent on the northeast corner of the lot, about two feet in from the line to give a little walking distance around the edge of our space. I took the northwest corner and Jason and Anna set up on the southeast corner. We all copied Dwayne and Tia, leaving some room around the edge. The centre and southwest corner we would use for cooking, eating, and relaxing.

By the time we finished setting up, we were all hungry and ready for a big meal. We waved to Bel on the way out and drove back to town, parking in one of the many spaces that lined the town square. We walked up the street, taking note of the various shops and restaurants — and by "the various," I really mean "the few." There was one men's and two women's clothing stores, a bakery, a couple of pubs, Annie's family restaurant, a hardware store, a pharmacy, the bank, the sheriff's office and jail, the courthouse, and the supermarket. The typical shops you would expect to see in a small town. I also noticed a line of food trucks at the edge of town, down by another bar. I wondered if they were to stay there or if they would eventually move down to the concert grounds.

We decided on Annie's, figuring the pubs would be rowdy and loud. We needed a quiet place to eat a good meal so we could get back to our tents to sleep. I would have skipped dinner altogether and just eaten a bag of chips, I was so tired, but the rest wanted a real meal. I was eager to see the town, so I didn't object. I wanted another look at the funeral home to see if it was as creepy as I'd thought on the way in.

Inside, Annie's was like just about every other family-owned small restaurant in North America. There were oversized booths that lined the perimeter and a row of tables down the centre of the floor. The colour scheme was comprised of black and white checked floors, red tabletops, and red vinyl upholstery on the chairs and booths. There was a small counter with stools across the back and a service window into the kitchen. The room was longer than it was wide. The lone cash register was at the back counter. There was a newer wireless POS machine beside it. A sign just inside the door invited us to seat ourselves.

We sat at an oversized booth, opposite the door and about halfway down the restaurant. I was surprised to see that the restaurant was almost full, even at this late hour. I imagined that most of the people inside were here for the concert, either as staff or as audience. Service might be slow, and the atmosphere was louder than we had hoped, but busy also meant hot, fresh food. I hoped it would arrive before I fell asleep.

Our server introduced herself as Sally. "I'll give you guys a few minutes to look over the menu. Can I get you something to drink?" she asked.

Tia piped up, "Do you guys serve a good milkshake? If so, I'd like a chocolate."

"Well only the biggest ones in town, doll!" Sally responded. That got us all excited and each of us ordered one. Tia and Jason ordered chocolate, Anna and Dwayne got strawberry, and I ordered a vanilla. Sally returned to the table with five tall glasses filled with the sweet treats and five silver tumblers half full of what wouldn't fit in the glass. So far it was the best thing that had happened that day.

I looked at the menu. There was nothing special about it: your usual assortment of hot and cold sandwiches, pizza, lasagna, fish and chips. Aside from the milkshakes, the beverages included soft drinks, coffee, and tea. They also served several local beers, but with Tia being under twenty-one, the legal age in Maine, no one even gave them a second thought. I personally chose not to, but I knew the others occasionally had a drink at home, where the drinking age was nineteen. I appreciated that although Jason and Anna, both twenty-two, and Dwayne, twenty-one, all could have ordered drinks, they chose instead to ensure that Tia felt part of the group.

Sally returned to the table, smiling. "All set?" she asked.

"Is the fish and chips haddock or cod or something else?" Once I determined it was indeed haddock, my favourite for fish and chips, I ordered a two-piece, hold the tartar sauce as I was allergic to mayonnaise. Jason had the hot hamburger sandwich with extra gravy, Dwayne got the lasagna, Tia ordered a pepperoni pizza for one, and Anna went for a chicken Caesar salad.

After we ordered, we turned our attention to the festival. "I think the first thing we should do tomorrow is check out the festival grounds. Stake out where the stage is, where the entrances are and all that, so we can have a game plan for Wednesday's opening concert." Jason started. "If there is lots of parking maybe we head over really early so we can get a great spot in front of the stage."

Tia asked, "What about taking a stroll through town and checking out the shops? I'd love a new outfit or something."

I was all for it. "I'd love to do that! If no one else is up for a shopping trip, I'll go. Plus, I need to find a shot glass, I've been collecting them since I was a kid when I thought they were 'kid glasses.' I have one from every place I've ever been."

Anna jumped in with, "Then let's make it a girl thing. No boys allowed. That way we can talk about you." Jason cast me a sideways glance that I pretended not to notice.

I wasn't sure if Jason had ever told Anna what really happened between us. By the look I just got, I guessed he hadn't. Perhaps now was the time? I definitely didn't want to hurt her, but she had a right to know, didn't she? And her best friend should be the one to tell her. I decided to fill her in, and if it hurt Jason, well, he had it coming.

We ate like we hadn't eaten in days. The fish was delicious, as were the fresh cut fries. There wasn't much talk, and everyone said their food was good. "Maybe we should come here for breakfast," Dwayne suggested. Everyone nodded agreement, but I was hoping to surprise them with a campfire breakfast, including some fresh trout if I could catch a couple before anyone got up. I was hoping to find Bel on the way back into the farm tonight to ask if she'd take me to one of the good fishing holes bright and early. Annie's was a good plan B, though.

Sally returned to the table to see if we wanted dessert. "We've got the best pie and chocolate cake in town!" she smiled.

Jason spoke up, "I think we are all sufficiently sufficed. Will you save us a slice for next time?"

She shook her head. "I'm sorry, I can't save you any." She paused. "Because it's made fresh every day!"

"What can you tell me about the funeral home?" I jumped in, "It looked pretty creepy on the way in."

"Well, when the Baptist Church closed a number of years ago, Mr. O'Reagan bought it. He built the morgue to join it to the old funeral home, and now the church is used as the funeral chapel. People don't go there unless they need to, and I don't mean just for funerals. Mr. O'Reagan is, well, he's a few bricks short of a load. He keeps to himself mostly. I think his only real friend is Sheriff Johnson. I'd steer clear of Mr. O'Reagan and the funeral home if I were you. Oh, another table is flagging me down. Gotta run. Enjoy your stay." And with that, she was off, leaving us to pay the cashier.

Jason paid for him and Anna, Tia paid for her and Dwayne, and I paid for myself. It sure would be nice to share bills like that again. Maybe it was time to open up and accept a date if someone asked. It wasn't the first time on this trip that I'd felt alone. I secretly wished things had been different with Jason. I wished he hadn't bolted, or that I had waited a little longer to tell him I wasn't pregnant, and then wouldn't have had to. Maybe I should have said "No" on Prom night. But that was all ancient history. Besides, he was with Anna now, and I was happy for her — at least, that's what I told myself. I hoped he had grown up and wouldn't leave her the way he'd left me. I was having a hard time with the whole situation.

Once we had paid (and left a very generous tip in case we came back), we got back in the car and headed to the farm.

As we passed the funeral home for the fourth time that day, I noted the few dim lights on inside.

"Don't you think that the funeral home looks creepy?" I said to my friends. "It looks like Freddy Krueger could jump right out of one of those windows!"

I got a few chuckles, but Tia leaned back and said, "I think you're right. It definitely looks spooky."

We arrived back at the farm, and Jason stopped at the gate when I told him I wanted to talk to Bel for a minute. She was still there in the booth and looked up from her book when we pulled in. The light from the single bulb over her head showed a big smile when she spotted me walking towards her. "Hey Bel!" I called. "How late are you out here?"

"Just until ten." She responded. "Can I help you with anything?"

I told her I was wondering if she could meet me early and show me the fishing holes.

"I'm hoping to catch a few fish before anyone gets up to surprise them with breakfast." She agreed to swing by my tent at six a.m. to take me across to the fishing holes. She even offered to bring along a few of her favourite lures to "ensure my success."

I climbed back into the car with a "Home, James!" and we went to the parking lot. As we parked, I looked towards where I thought our tents were, and low and behold, there was a soft, purple glow. Jason saw me staring and said "I brought some coloured glow sticks with me to mark our tent. I figured it could be hard to find in the dark." I thought to myself, "That's my man," and then caught myself. No, it wasn't. He was Anna's man.

"That was so smart, baby. Thanks for thinking of that." Anna kissed him on the cheek and headed off towards the light. We all followed, with me trailing behind.

I crawled into my tent and laid on my camping mattress. I was so tired I thought about not even changing out of my clothes. I did, though, and was soon snuggled into my sleeping bag. I thought about tomorrow, and about talking to Anna. Her dating Jason had definitely put a strain on our friendship. As best friends we had always supported each other. On the other hand, I was jealous — jealous that she looked so happy with my ex. I suddenly realized I missed him. I fell asleep wondering how to reconcile all of these feelings so that I could be happy again. So that I could finally move on. I yawned, stretched, and went to sleep. Bel would be here all too soon to take me fishing.

CHAPTER 5

I HEARD BEL QUIETLY whispering my name outside the tent.

"I'll be right out," I whispered. I quickly dressed in a pair of army green capris and muted yellow top and emerged with my fishing pole in hand.

"Good morning, sleepyhead," Bel smiled. As we quietly weaved through the maze of tents, I noticed that she was taller than me by about an inch, putting her at about 5 foot 9. She had a great smile, walked with a light step, and seemed very happy. Once we cleared the tents she turned.

"Did you have a good sleep?"

I chuckled. "Not nearly long enough. After our day yesterday, I think I could have slept until noon!" When she asked what was so rough about it, I filled her in with a few of the details.

"Oh dear," she said. "Well, I hope the rest of your trip goes better — starting right now!" We had arrived at a small beach on the edge of a lake that had some grass poking through the surface. "There's a hole in here that's deeper than it looks, and the lake trout like to come in to feed off the minnows and bugs that land in among the grasses. I bet you catch all you need for breakfast," she predicted.

I set about expanding my fishing pole and was just about to fit a lure onto it when she said, "Here, use this." She produced a small lure that had a yellow and orange belly and a brown top. "Thanks," I smiled.

I cast the lure out across the water and began to reel it in. All at once, BAM! A fish bit my lure. I snapped the end of the rod back to set the hook and began to slowly reel in the fish. It put up a big fight. I won a little, it took a little, I won a little more. I laughed, "This must be a monster!"

Bel was smiling from ear to ear. She clapped her hands and squealed, "I knew this was the spot for you! And that lure never fails."

After wrestling with the fish for about ten minutes, I finally landed the biggest trout I had ever seen outside a supermarket. It was huge! One more fish like this and I'd have enough to feed all of us, and maybe even have leftovers. It didn't take long to hook my second fish, another large trout, only slightly smaller than the first. I set about cleaning the fish on a rock with my jackknife. Leaving the head, guts and scales for the scavengers, Bel and I headed back to the farm.

"Thanks for showing me such a great fishing hole, Bel," I said. "I really appreciate that. Why don't you join us for breakfast? I'm going to make some eggs and toast to go with the fish. I'm sure the gang would love to get to know you better."

Bel hesitated. "Are you sure? I wouldn't want to impose. Papa says I shouldn't bother our guests."

I laughed. "It's not bothering us if you've been invited! Tell your dad it would bother us if you *didn't* join us. Come on, you can help me cook."

We noticed that people were starting to stir, so we weren't as quiet as we made our way through the field to our campsite. Dwayne and Tia emerged from their tent as we got the fire going, and Jason and Anna joined us as the smell of fresh fish and eggs began to fill the air. My melancholy from the night before lifted as my new friend Bel and I prepared a delicious breakfast. It was a great morning.

Anna insisted she and Jason take care of cleanup. Bel thanked us for breakfast but said she needed to get back to her duties on the farm. She had already milked the cows before coming to take me fishing, and now she needed to clean up the barn and feed the chickens. We could already see her dad out on the tractor, checking on the crops and setting the irrigation pipes.

Shoot! I thought. I had meant to ask Bel about the funeral home and see if she had anything else to add. Sally had left more questions in my head than she'd answered. It still freaked me out how creepy it looked.

"Okay, the dishes are done and our bellies are full. Let's head into town for our girls' day!" Anna said. "I'm excited to see what this place has to offer."

"Yes, I want to spend some money on myself," giggled Tia.

"What are the boys going to do this morning?" I asked.

"Well, Beth, I think Dwayne and I will tidy camp a little, and maybe go for a swim in the lake — if we can find the beach. Then we'll have lunch ready for you ladies when you return, say . . . one o'clock?"

In unison we said, almost singing, "See you then. Bye!" And we were off.

On the way out, Tia pointed out how many more people had moved in since we arrived the previous night. A few must have come in while we slept or early this morning. There were more cars at the gate waiting to come in. Bel was going to have a busy day. She had told me they were expecting all twelve hundred sites to be full, some with six or seven people on them. In all, her family was expecting just over five thousand "house guests," about one tenth of the festival attendees. Getting a shower was going to take some advanced planning.

We drove to the opposite end of Main Street and parked. Our plan was to walk down one side of the road to the end of town and then come back up the other side. Tia didn't want to miss "any opportunity to buy something cool to remember the trip by. And I want a new outfit." I was glad to be out alone with the girls. It lifted my spirits. Anna and I hadn't spent a lot of time one-on-one since she and Jason had started dating. As much as I hated to admit it, their relationship was a wasp sting to my soul.

We got out of the car after we parked on the west end of Main Street. We could hear the many volunteers and employees getting the festival grounds set up for the following evening's first concert. The gates were set to open at four p.m., and the concert by Justin Bieber would start at seven.

It was only nine thirty, so most shops had yet to open, but amazing smells were coming from Bill's Bakery and Coffee Shop. In spite of our big breakfast, my stomach growled for whatever it was I was smelling. That, and coffee. No one in our group had packed any coffee. I would have to stop at the supermarket.

In the bakery we were greeted by Kim, one of the servers. She took us to a seat deep inside the busy shop and handed us each a small menu. One look at it, and I knew we would be back. There were muffins, croissants, cinnamon buns, cookies and more. All were baked fresh daily. All the coffee was roasted and ground on site. There were so many different blends to choose from I didn't know where to start. There were also espresso drinks, steamers, and teas. I was deep in thought when I heard Kim say, "Sorry for the wait. It's a busy morning already and one of our servers called in sick. Have you had a chance to look at the menu?"

"Oh my gosh, Kim," said Tia. "Everything smells so delicious! I hardly know where to begin. What do you suggest?"

Kim paused for just a moment. "I would suggest the cinnamon buns. They just came out of the oven and are still warm. You can get them plain, with cream cheese frosting, or with a buttercream style frosting. I'll warn you they are quite large, though."

I looked at Tia and Anna and jumped in. "I think I speak for all of us when I say we'll take three! Mine just plain please." Anna wanted hers with the cream cheese frosting and Tia decided she would try one with the buttercream so we could all try each one. "Now what about the coffee?" I asked. "I like something bright and flavourful but without the bitterness of a dark roast."

Kim smiled. "I know exactly what you need: our Morning Mountain Blend. It's a favourite of our locals here in Harrington. It'll wake you up with its bold flavours but won't disappoint by leaving a bitter aftertaste. One of my customers swears a little coffee bean jumps up and slaps him across the face every time he drinks it. Might I also suggest a little steamed milk in it for some extra body without interfering with its flavour?"

I liked this girl, a lot. "Oh, that sounds delicious. Please bring me a large one of those."

Anna and Tia weren't as fussy as I was about coffee. Tia ordered a London Fog (Earl Grey tea with steamed milk), while Anna ordered a Breakfast Blend with cream and two sugars.

The cinnamon buns turned out to be even better, and bigger, than promised. I mean these things were to die for. I told Kim to tell Bill he had nice buns. She giggled and said she would. Then she told me Bill was her dad, and he'd heard it before but always liked to hear it again.

We didn't finish the cinnamon buns as they were simply too big, especially after breakfast, but Kim was happy to box up the leftovers. We bought more on the way out to take back for the guys, and us, for later. We took them back to the car, so we didn't have to carry them around town, and then set out to explore.

As we passed the bakery again, Kim waved from the window. I would definitely be back there for a snack and a coffee. Maybe she knew something about the funeral home.

Just past Bill's was a hair salon. The sign on the door read "Joyce will be back at 11:00." Beside Joyce's was a convenience store. We went in figuring they might have souvenirs. I saw a shelf with some shot glasses on it and made a beeline for them.

"Beth, how do I look?" I turned and saw Anna wearing a bright yellow sun hat and oversized sunglasses. The hat read "Town of Harrington, Home of MAINESTOCK 2019." I laughed and told her, "You look maaavelous, dahling!" I went back to the shot glasses but decided that I would wait and see what else I could find in town.

We walked further up and crossed Maple Street, a residential street with a volunteer fire department on the corner. It had two bay doors on the left and a door in the middle with what was likely office space and storage for gear and equipment. The sign out front read "Welcome to Mainestock." Next was a vacant lot, and then we entered the town square. Across the street from the Town Hall was a small park between lanes of traffic. At the centre was a beautiful fountain surrounded by park benches. It reminded me of one of the picturesque small towns in a Hallmark movie. There was little cherub on a pedestal in the centre with water flowing from his penis. It reminded me of the one we used to have in the fountain in Fredericton, which the locals had nicknamed "Freddy the Nude Dude." That is, before someone stole it in the middle of the night! There were coins in the fountain. An assortment of shrubs and a maple tree at each end cast beautiful shade.

Next to the parking lot was a small hotel. It didn't appear to have a name, just a sign hanging vertically on the building that read "Hotel." That was it. Next, we found Amy's Amazing Outfits, a women's clothing store. Tia ran to the door. "Come on ladies. I'm going to find me a nice outfit to surprise Dwayne with." Then she disappeared through the door with Anna and I right behind her.

The shop was small but filled with great clothes. I was surprised by the quality and variety, not to mention styles. I don't know what I expected but it wasn't a store filled with the latest fashions. Tia played fashionista for about half an hour. She tried on tops and pants and skirts and dresses, each one looking better than the last. Finally, she had a gorgeous little outfit assembled. A flowing white cotton skirt that stopped just above the knee, a cute light-green top with a flower pattern around a scooped neck that fell off the shoulder, and a pair of leather sandals that had a beautiful green flowery design resting mid-foot. They matched the top perfectly. Her light brown skin made the outfit really pop. I found a great light-blue top that Anna said matched my eyes perfectly. Anna decided to save her money in case she found something else or wanted to buy extra concert souvenirs. She said she could always come back.

Once we paid for our wonderful finds, we continued up the street. The Spencer Hotel was next, and then Pine Street, lined with homes. On the corner across the street was the funeral home, O'Reagan's. It looked just as foreboding as before. I couldn't put my finger on why it made my skin crawl. On its own, it was a very large century home with a big addition on the back, which I assumed was the crematorium Sally told me about, or maybe casket storage. The addition linked the house to the church next door, which still bore the sign that read Harrington First Baptist Church. Why would they need to say First Baptist in this small town? I wondered. The church had a high, sharply sloped roof with what I thought could be the original bell tower, long since boarded up.

A single car, a blue 2019 BMW 8 series convertible, sat in the funeral home's yard. As I looked at the car, a man came from the house across the street. He was tall, I guessed about six feet four, with fire-red hair. He looked about forty, with what I would call a high-end dadbod — you know the type: bulging biceps, a nice chest, but a little belly to go with it.

As he got to the car, the tall man noticed us on the corner. He smiled and waved. A shiver ran down my spine. I didn't know why — perhaps because we were standing in the shade of the hotel. Or maybe he just had a bad vibe about him. I guessed he was the funeral director.

As he drove passed us, he called, "Welcome to Harrington. I hope you enjoy the festival!" Then he turned down the road to Millinocket. I watched him go because I loved his car. When I turned back to the funeral home, I could have sworn I saw a little boy in the window, but then he was gone. *It was just a shadow*, I told myself.

We crossed Main Street and started back towards our car. The first business we came to was The Spruce Bar and Grill. It appeared to be upscale but inviting. I put it on our list of spots to eat. The Irish Inn was next, almost directly across from The Spencer Hotel. Then came the town square again, with the Courthouse, sheriff's station and town jail all but joined together. As we got to the sheriff's station, the door opened, and an officer stepped out and ran right into Anna, knocking her to the ground.

"Oh, I'm so sorry!" the officer blushed, bending down to help her up. "I was stuck in my head and didn't even see you there. Please, accept my apology. I'm Sheriff Alex Johnson. You must be here for the festival."

"I'm ok," said Anna as she picked herself up off the ground. "My name is Anna, and these are my friends, Beth and Tia. And yes, we're here for the festival. Just taking a little time today to explore town."

"Well, I hope you enjoy it. If you need anything, please come by my office and I, or my staff, will be glad to help. Now, if you'll excuse me," he said, "I need to get down to the festival grounds to do a security walk-through." And with that, he got into his patrol car and drove off down the street.

I glanced down at my watch and noticed that it was just after twelve thirty. "We need to get back; the guys will have lunch ready for us."

"Then I guess we get to do another girls' morning tomorrow to explore the rest of town!" exclaimed Tia, and then she began to run. I looked at Anna. She looked at me. We smiled and ran after her.

"Wait for us!" Anna shouted.

CHAPTER 6

THE GUYS HAD the camp stove hooked up and were cooking hamburgers for lunch. "Well, there you are!" Dwayne called out when he saw us. "You're just in time."

Jason looked up and said, "Hey, babe!" as he smiled at Anna. He used to call me "babe." I felt a twinge in my heart and instantly chastised myself for thinking like that. He was with Anna now and they were happy. Be happy for them, I thought. Besides, the burgers smelled delicious, and I was hungry again after all that walking.

"We brought a surprise!" I said, pulling the Bill's Bakery bag out from behind my back. "Fresh cinnamon buns for dessert, and they are delicious!"

The burgers tasted fabulous. Jason remembered how I liked them and cooked them perfectly. A nice thick patty, slightly pink in the middle with American cheese melted on top. He put just a little bit of mustard, ketchup, and a single pickle right in the middle, so that I got a little hint of the sweet and sour cucumber with each bite that didn't overpower the taste of the beef. What can I say, I love a nice bit of cow. A girl needs her vices, doesn't she?

Anna and I washed the dishes using water the guys had collected earlier from the lake and put through the little water filter Jason had brought with him.

"Ok, I need to go for a quick shower," I said. "I didn't get a chance before I caught breakfast. Can you give me thirty minutes before we head over to see the festival grounds?"

I walked across the growing makeshift campground, dodging campsites and campers who were busy moving in and setting up. I figured the water in the shower would never be hotter than in the middle of the day, after the sun had had time to warm the water in the black hoses on the roof. I was right. The water was almost as hot as it was at home. I even needed to add a little cold so that I wouldn't burn myself. I let the water roll over me for a bit before I grabbed the shampoo and washed my hair. I had remembered to bring my razor with me and made quick work of shaving. I paused briefly as I shaved around the scar on my calf where my bicycle pedal had torn out a good chunk of flesh when I was a kid. My parents had taken me to the Chalmers Hospital where I got twelve stiches. One of the many small battle wounds I'd received during my adventures.

I got back to find the gang ready to go, sitting in camp chairs, talking and laughing. "OK, I'm good to go," I said as I tossed my shampoo into my tent and hung up my towel on the makeshift clothesline we had put up between tents.

Tia jumped up, "Last one to the car buys treats at Bill's!" She laughed as she took off running. I didn't think I could eat another cinnamon bun — but maybe a chocolate chip cookie, I smiled to myself. I looked at Anna and we both ran after Tia, leaving the guys to wonder what had just happened. Dwayne arrived last, a split second later than Jason, and agreed that he would buy treats for dessert on the way back from the festival grounds.

We drove through town, and I noticed that there were several cars in the parking lot of the funeral home. Mr. O'Reagan stood there holding the door open as people went in. A shiver ran down my spine.

Traffic slowed as we approached the local fairgrounds, which had been upgraded for the festival. There was a giant grandstand that looked to be permanent. It was positioned so that you couldn't see the front from the road, but you could see it from anywhere within the gates. One crew was raising lights at the front and back of the stage while another assembled a large array of speakers, hooking them up to some of the scaffolding high overhead.

To one side there was a transport truck. I watched the driver get out and push some buttons and I was amazed as the side panel started to slide up. Jason pulled over and we all watched as the bed of the truck slowly transformed into a covered stage. Light trusses were already in place. The stage looked ready for the crew to set up the lights and speakers. It was really cool. I figured this was the stage where the second-tier acts would perform so that the main artists would be sure their sound levels stayed correct.

We drove up to a parking lot. We walked around to see the points of entry relative to the stage and to scope out the best seats. Dwayne had suggested we sit near the sound booth. He told us that was where the best sound would be as the techs always mixed for their ears.

The mainstage entrance was heavily guarded by security and marked with the sign "Staff Only. ID Required." It was busy with staff coming and going. Behind the stage were dozens of trailers. I wondered if these were dressing rooms for the artists, or if they were sleeping quarters for the crew.

We crossed to the fence near the staff entrance. There were food trucks lining the perimeter of the fairgrounds, far from the stages. We saw medical and water distribution tents. Water was "free" but I'm sure the cost was built into the tickets. I also noted that there were two "blue cities," one on each end of the line of food trucks. These were the rows of portable toilets.

"Ok, so what do you guys want to do now?" Jason asked after we had finished scoping out the fairgrounds. "The afternoon is still young."

"What about the old town?" Tia suggested. "I was reading up on the area, and if we keep going down Main St. past the turn for the farm, we get to the site of the old town. Apparently, there are still some of the old buildings and stuff there, as well as the cemetery. I think it would be fun!"

"Then, let's go!" I exclaimed, always ready for an adventure. "I think it would be cool to see a real live ghost town. Maybe we'll even see a ghost!" I laughed as I climbed into the Pilot.

CHAPTER 7

JASON LET DWAYNE drive this time. The old town was about two miles east of the turn off to the farm. It looked like everyone had just up and left one day. There were several buildings still standing, including the sheriff's station, fire station, a few shops and an O'Reagan's funeral home, presumably the original one. The sign on the front was similar, with the name "O'Reagan's" featured prominently.

Dwayne parked in front of the old town hall.

"Where do we go first?" asked Anna.

"How about we start with the town hall?" Dwayne replied. "That is, if we can even get in. Everything might be locked up."

I bounced up the big staircase, turned the knob, and the door opened. "Looks like we have an invitation to go exploring," I called to the group, smiling. I didn't wait for them to follow. I simply stepped over the threshold.

I was standing in a large entryway with a wide hall in front of me and stairs that led up to the left. It was a little dark inside as the lower windows had all been boarded up and the only light came from the smaller windows up high and the skylight that was over the stairs and hallway. A sign on a door to the right said Reception: Please Enter, so I did, instinctively closing the door behind me. In front of me was a long desk with a hinged section to allow access. I lifted it and went behind the desk. I heard everyone else coming through the door, so I quietly placed the top back down and ducked behind the desk.

"Beth," Anna called, "where did you go?" I quietly giggled, waiting for my chance to scare them.

"Beth," this time it was Jason. "Come on Beth, quit playing games. It's spooky enough in here without you scaring us."

I heard the door to the reception area open but kept quiet, supressing another giggle. I heard the floor creek. "Beth, are you in here?" It was Tia. Another creek in the floor. "I don't think she's in here, guys, maybe she went upstairs."

"Maybe she's in one of those offices behind the counter and didn't hear us." This time it was Dwayne. "Come on Jason, let's look."

I heard footsteps and jumped up from behind the counter. "BOO!" I yelled. Tia and Anna screamed and ran from the room. Jason leaped back and hit Dwayne in the chest with his shoulder, almost knocking him over. I laughed hard.

"Dang, Beth! You scared the crap out of us. I think I peed a little," Anna exclaimed, then began to laugh. Tia peeked back in the room and started to laugh too. Soon we were all laughing.

After a minute or two, Jason spoke up. "Okay, pact time, no more scaring each other."

"Actually," I laughed, "I think it would be fun to play hide and seek. Who's in?"

"Maybe after we explore some more. I think we need to check things out first. Some of these old buildings could be dangerous," Dwayne cautioned. "After that, I'm game."

We went from door to door on the main floor and found nothing of interest, just a few desks, a broken office chair, and lots and lots of cobwebs. The black rice-sized droppings told us rats or mice were living here. We didn't see any creatures, but I didn't think anyone had been in here sprinkling the place with black rice.

Dwayne led us to the stairs. "The stairs may not be safe, so I'll go first. I'm the heaviest, so if anyone is going to go through, it'll be me. That way no one else will get hurt." He was making a nice show of bravery for Tia. I thought it was sweet, and apparently, so did she. Her hero. I smiled.

It was considerably brighter upstairs without boards on the windows. We went from room to room but didn't find much more than we had on the first floor. A couple of desks, another office chair, more mouse droppings and cobwebs. Suddenly, I heard a scream and thought Anna or Tia had been hurt. I ran from the room into the hall just as Jason came running, screaming, "Get it off! Get it off!" He was wiping at his face and neck. There were about a dozen spiders, a couple of them pretty big, crawling across his neck, back and hair. I brushed them off and he immediately gathered himself like nothing had happened. "What?" he shrugged, as we all laughed. He was clearly posturing for Anna's benefit.

I laughed, "Jason, I've never heard you scream like a girl before. I thought it was Anna or Tia!" He shot me a subtle but dirty look, and I said nothing more.

Next door to the town hall, the sheriff's station was also unlocked. The side door led us behind the front desk into what appeared to have been a small bullpen. There were three desks. I sat at one and put my feet up on it. "Howdy pardners," I said in my best imitation of a country drawl. "What brings y'all to these here parts?" Everyone laughed at how bad my accent was.

There were three jail cells at the back of the building, all open. Each one had a sink–toilet combination and a concrete slab that could be used as a bed if a mattress were on top. I had heard how small cells could be, but only from movies and TV.

We went from building to building until we came to O'Reagan's. We stopped out front and no one made a move to try the door. I was as creeped out as anyone, but there we were, standing outside the last building. Was anyone brave enough to touch the door? Was I? Then, somehow, I sucked it up and reached for the door. Jason grabbed my hand, "Are you sure?"

I got a little defensive. "Why not? It's only an abandoned building. It's not like it's haunted or anything. I hope," I added under my breath.

I grabbed the door handle and turned. It wasn't locked either, or maybe the lock had been broken. It seemed odd that all of these buildings were left unlocked, even if the town was abandoned. I took a deep breath and pushed on the door. It swung open. None of us moved. We all peered inside for a moment, and then I took a tentative step inside. Everyone followed me closely. When I stopped, they bumped into me and I tumbled forward into the lobby, nearly landing on my face. I rolled over and looked up at them and we all broke out laughing.

"Are you ok?" asked Anna.

"I'm fine, just a little dusty." I got up and dusted myself off. "I don't know what we were scared of, it's just an empty building." I looked around and took in the room. A sign above the door on the right read "A" and the one above the left-hand door read "B." Both rooms were empty except for the carpeting that was torn and coming up in places. They each had peeling, identical wallpaper and wall sconces. Each had its own fireplace, but I hadn't seen any chimneys outside, so I figured they were just for show.

We walked down a hall and came to another door marked Office. A matching door with the nameplate reading Patrick O'Reagan was directly across from it. The office had a built-in, two-tier desk where a receptionist would sit, and an old filing cabinet that lay on its side with two of its four drawers open and empty. Patrick O'Reagan's office had built-in shelving along one side, some vertical blinds hanging from the window, and an old black and white picture of a handsome man in his forties on the wall. I thought he looked familiar. The caption underneath read: Patrick O'Reagan. Then it hit me.

"Hey Anna, Tia, doesn't that look like the tall guy we saw this morning at the funeral home — the one in town?" They both took a closer look and nodded in agreement.

"I bet he's this guy's grandson or something," Tia suggested.

At the end of the hall was one more door: The Mortuary. We looked at each other to see who would go in first. I made up my mind that it wouldn't be me this time. My spider senses were tingling again, and my skin was starting to crawl. I didn't know what it was about O'Reagan's. I'd been in many funeral homes for funerals and visitations and it had never bothered me. Something just didn't feel right.

Dwayne stepped forward and pushed open the door. He took a step in, and then another. Jason was right behind him. Then me, then Tia. Anna brought up the rear. We saw a wall of doors like you would see in a movie morgue. They looked like the walk-in fridge doors we had when I worked at McDonald's, only smaller, about three feet square. There were two rows of three. Two sinks stood against one wall and there were three overturned metal tables on the tile floor. Dwayne picked one up and set it upright. It was an odd table with a depression running the length of it, kind of like a half pipe only shallow. Then along each edge was a channel or ditch that ran across the end of the table and down both sides. There was a hole in one end. Jason went over and opened one of the doors and pulled out a tray. Thank God it was empty!

"Jason, why are you opening those?" Anna gasped! "There were dead people in there. What if there still are?" Jason stopped opening the doors, but I needed to see inside.

"I'm sure they're all empty," I said, as I opened them each, one by one. They were all unoccupied.

We had explored the whole place by now and headed back towards the front door. On the way by Patrick O'Reagan's office I peaked in. I did a double take. The picture was no longer on the wall. I stopped and looked, thinking I had mistaken what wall it was on, but all four walls were empty.

"Hey guys!" I called, but they were already out the door. I was totally creeped out now and got out of there in a hurry. Where had the picture gone? Had someone snuck in while we were at the morgue and removed it? It couldn't have just disappeared.

As I turned back towards the door, I bumped into someone. I screamed and jumped back.

"I'm sorry to have scared you." It was the tall guy from the funeral parlour. "I'm Mr. O'Reagan, Conor O'Reagan. I own the funeral home in town. I used to own this one too. I guess I still do, but when the town moved, we all just picked up and relocated. Seeing you in here made me remember to come get the picture of my grandfather." He smiled as he held up the picture to his face. "I look a lot like him."

"Sss . . . Sorry I bumped into you," I stammered. "We were just looking around. We didn't hurt anything."

"Not to worry, dear. It's not like there's anything valuable left. Even the ghosts seem to have packed up and moved into town with me."

"Ghosts?" I asked.

"Surely you must have heard the tale of the little boy that haunts the funeral home — Michael? At least that's the rumour. I've never personally seen him, but others swear to his existence. Maybe you should stop in sometime for a tour, so you can see a working funeral home and not just this old, abandoned building."

"I'm not sure we'll have time. We have the music festival." I paused. "Well, I have to run, my friends are waiting." I scooted past him. As I got to the door I looked back, and he was nowhere to be seen. He must have gone into another room, I thought.

I caught up with everyone on the street. "What took you so long?" Tia asked.

"I ran into the funeral director. He told me that the ghosts had followed him to the new place, and that there is supposed to the ghost of a little boy that haunts the funeral home. He said he never saw it but that others have. He even invited us to see the place."

"The funeral director was in there? Why didn't any of us see him?" Jason asked.

"Yes, he was, but I have no idea where he went."

"Well, we didn't see him come out. He must still be in there," Anna stated. "Let's go ask him more about the town."

"You guys go ahead," I replied. "That guy gives me the creeps. I'll wait here."

Everyone went in but Anna, who stayed to keep me company. We'd only waited a couple of minutes when everyone came out. "There's no one in there," Dwayne reported. "Are you sure he was there?"

"Yes, I'm sure. I talked to him."

"Well, there's no one in there now. Let's go."

We turned to head back to the car when I spotted a hearse and several people, including Conor O'Reagan, at the cemetery. As I was looking, the tall man turned and spotted us. He gave a slight wave and then turned back to the burial he was attending to. Everyone turned to look at me. I just stood there, mouth open, wondering how he got by us.

CHAPTER 8

BACK AT THE campsite, we were tired and hungry. We opted for cold cuts on some buns we'd brought and sat back in our camp chairs to relax. The campground was pretty much full now. Dwayne and Tia set about starting a fire. I took a walk over to the restrooms. On the way back, I saw Bel driving a four-wheeler with a trailer on the back. She was going through the campground changing out all the garbage cans.

"Hi Bel!" I hollered. She turned and smiled, then made a tight turnaround and drove over to say hello.

"Hi Beth! How was your first full day in Harrington?"

"We had a great day." I filled Bel in on our shopping trip this morning. She said she couldn't wait to see my new top. Then I told her about scouting out the festival. "What are the buses usually like?" I asked her. "We were thinking we would drive over in the morning to avoid the crowds on the bus and to be sure to get there first."

"That's not a bad idea. The buses can get pretty full. I wish I could go, but I need to work. Besides, we don't go into town much. We mostly keep to ourselves. Dad says it's safer that way," responded Bel.

While the last comment struck me as odd, I didn't pry. I assumed they had their reasons. I had heard about Immigration and Customs Enforcement and how poorly undocumented people were treated here in the US. I didn't want to open a sore conversation or sound too nosy. "Why don't you swing by our site after you're done?" I invited. "We are going to sit around the campfire and talk, maybe even sing a campfire song or two."

"I would love that!" Bel gushed. "Let me finish up the last of my work and I'll be over. Maybe an hour?"

"Perfect," I told her. "See you then."

When I returned to the campsite, the fire was going really well. The couples were cozied up next to each other and my chair was sitting there by itself, waiting for me. In that moment I decided it was definitely time to say "yes" the next time a good guy invited me out on a date. No more waiting around until I was set in a career.

I took my seat and told them, "Bel is going to join us in a bit. I ran into her near the restrooms. I hope you guys don't mind. She seems so nice, and a little lonely." No one objected, which was good, because she was on her way shortly.

"I was just saying that we should go into town for breakfast in the morning. Maybe we could hit up Annie's or Bill's Bakery," Anna said.

"Sure," I replied. "Both spots were delicious and had good service. Bill's had those great buns, but at Annie's we can get a whole breakfast."

"Breakfast in town it is, then," smiled Tia. "And maybe I can get into that other ladies' shop we saw?" Anna and I looked at each other and laughed. We were learning more and more about Tia. Number one: she liked to shop!

It wasn't long before Bel showed up and sat down on the ground beside me. Dwayne poked at the fire and got up to add another log. "So, Bel, how long have you and your family lived here in Harrington?" he asked.

"About fifteen years I think," Bel let us know. "I was just little." She looked at Anna. "Papi was looking for a spot out of the way to farm and saw that this piece of land was for sale cheap. He had been saving all his life to buy land of his own. He promised Mama that he would provide for her, and this was his way, to grow all the food we needed and then sell enough to buy clothes and things. Now, thanks to this festival and the campers, we are doing very well. I heard Papi say that the money from the campers pays all the bills for the year. Even the fee he pays to the town."

"So where did you go to school? We haven't seen one since we arrived," said Anna.

"There's an elementary school and a middle school. They are at the north end of town on Mallard Lane, off Main Street. Both schools are rather small with many split classes. Starting in grade eight, students are bussed into Millinocket to Stearns High School, home of the Minutemen!" she laughed. "I was home-schooled until high school and then took the bus with the rest of the kids from town. We catch the bus at the town hall at seven each morning and then it drops us off at four thirty every afternoon. If it snows, we get a day off, which happens quite a bit from December to March. I actually just graduated in June. Papi says I should go away to college and get a degree. He says I should make something of myself. I tell him I want to help with the farm, at least for now. He wants me to get out of Harrington and do better than him. But I don't think he did so bad."

"So, what's it like growing up in such a small town, out here in the middle of nowhere?" I asked.

"It's ok," Bel remarked. "I have lots of work to do around the farm, helping Dad out. And then there's school, well, until now that is. I get to go fishing, hunting, and hiking, and we have a big screen TV and watch lots of movies and things. I also like to read."

"What about boys," Tia wanted to know. "Are there any cute guys around?"

Bel blushed a little, "Well there was one guy in my chemistry class at school, but he was from Millinocket. He called on me a couple of times, but Papi wasn't too keen on me dating a boy from the big city. But the folks around here are, well, different. None of us go into town more than necessary. I take fresh produce and meat to the market most days while Papi milks the cows, and Mama goes shopping in Millinocket once a week, but other than that we keep to ourselves. Someday I'm going to get out of here and meet a nice boy, and we'll get married and have a family."

I raised my cup of coffee. "Here's to that dream coming true!"

"I bet you've met a Bigfoot way out here." Dwayne joked.

"Do you mean a Sasquatch? If so, then yes, many times. We actually have a small family that seems to live nearby. They visit us often. Sometimes we see them, and other times we just see their tracks, or the animals let us know they're here. They smell really bad. Like the boy's locker room at school, only worse. They usually come and pick some fruit or vegetables from the garden. They killed a sheep once. That's why we only have cows and pigs."

Dwayne's jaw dropped and his eyes got big and round as Bel spoke. He looked at Jason and then at me and then Bel started to laugh, hard. And then we all got the joke and had a big laugh together. "I'm sorry to lead you all on," Bel continued to laugh. "I just couldn't resist. We get asked that at least ten times per festival."

Once we all stopped laughing, Bel said, "I do have a true story for you, though. No joking this time. If you want to hear it, that is. It's a ghost story."

Tia leaned in. "For real? A true ghost story? I want to hear!"

"What about the rest of you?" Bel asked, as we all nodded in response. "I'll start with a little town history first. Harrington was incorporated as a town in the summer of 1881. It was established in 1879 when the first people moved in seeking the rich natural resources here. It was rumoured there was gold in the streams, but after a year of searching, none had been found. Most people moved on, but some decided to stay. The soil in the clearings is rich with nutrients and crops grow well." She motioned to her farm. "The streams and lakes are full of fish and the forest is full of wildlife. By 1880, many of our predecessors had built homes and a small downtown was built. What is now the old ghost town northeast of here.

"Patrick O'Reagan opened the first funeral home. His great-great-grandson Conor runs it now like his father Sean before him. Sheriff Johnson's family was here then as well. Rumour has it they were slaves to one of the original families, though I don't know which one. The current Sheriff Johnson, Alex, is the second Sheriff Johnson we've had. His father was sheriff before him, but he died some time ago. Alex and Conor went to school together and are still friends.

They both sit on the town's council." As Bel talked about the funeral home, I was on the edge of my seat, hoping for lots of detail. I still had that creepy feeling deep in my gut. I just felt that something was off. But then again, you had to be off to want to work in a funeral home, didn't you?

Bel continued, "As the town began to grow, council thought that it would be better to move it up the road, a little closer to the highway that led to Millinocket, and a little closer to the lake. The fire department recommended this for the proximity to water, should there ever be a big fire like in Chicago. A big town meeting was held, and it apparently became quite a contentious issue if you listen to the townsfolks. The town eventually moved to where it is now in 1910. The Baptists decided it would be good to have their church right on the town square. It's two doors down from the police station."

I remembered running by it that morning as we chased Tia to the car.

"Patrick O'Reagan eventually arranged to buy the church from them to use as the funeral home chapel. He also bought the parsonage next door to use as the funeral home itself. Over the years it's seen several expansions, the last one about ten years ago, after we moved here. They expanded the crematorium and the morgue, which is now used occasionally by some vets from around the area to do animal autopsies."

"Necropsies." I corrected.

"That's the word!" she agreed. "Once in a while, if the morgue is full in Millinocket, or if someone here dies and the insurance company needs a cause of death or something, they send the coroner out here to do an autopsy and they use the funeral home. It's supposed to be state of the art. Conor and his wife live across the road, and he runs it. His wife Sarah is a computer security specialist. Now, for the good part. From the stories I hear, when Conor was first apprenticing with his dad, a young boy named Michael was pronounced dead by the local doctor. He had drowned in the lake when he was ice fishing in March. The ice can get soft that time of year, and even though the fishing huts need to be gone by the fifteenth, the season doesn't close until the end of the month. The boy went out and had caught a couple of fish, when the ice apparently gave way. Another fisherman saw him go under and tried to rescue him. It was over forty-five minutes by the time someone else had contacted the fire department and help arrived. Given the length of time he had been under and that there were no vital signs, the old doc said there was no way he would live. They took him to the funeral home and Conor was tasked with performing an embalming. His dad was with another family, so it was to be Conor's first solo embalming.

"When Conor began, he noticed that the boy was bleeding and thought nothing of it as some blood was expected, or so the story goes. But when the bleeding didn't stop, he panicked and instead of helping, he ran to get his dad. By the time they both got back, the boy was dead. The way I hear it, the boy must have woken up enough to move, as he had curled up into the fetal position."

"I don't know if I could keep working at the same job if it was me." I spoke. "That must have been horrible.

"It must have been," Bel continued. "The rest of the details are even fuzzier. I know there was an investigation and that no fault was found, or charges laid. Conor left town for a number of months. I heard he was in therapy for PTSD and stuff. I know the boy's dad was furious and died of a heart attack while marching up and down the town square, picketing and demanding Conor go to jail for murder. It is said that the boy, Michael, roams the halls of the funeral home so that he can prevent anyone else from dying there."

"I think I might have seen him," I exclaimed. "When we first got here, I saw a boy in the window looking at me. It was just for a second or two. I looked away, and when I looked back, he was gone."

"It was probably just some kid there with his parents while they made arrangements or something," Jason reassured me.

"But there were no cars in the parking lot," I countered.

"The town is so small they likely walked over. Remember that the funeral director was in the parking lot too."

"I think I'm not going to sleep very well tonight," mused Tia. "I'll be too scared."

"*You?* What about *me?*" I asked. "I'm the one sleeping alone. You have a big, strong, handsome man to snuggle and protect you all night long."

"You think I'm handsome? Thanks!" grinned Dwayne. I threw a marshmallow at him in protest.

"Oh, my goodness! It's almost midnight," declared Bel. "I need to get home and go to bed. I'm up at four thirty to help with chores before I'm needed here at the campground. It's always a crazy busy week. Have fun sleeping," she laughed.

"Thanks for the story," Jason paused. "I think."

I gave Bel a hug goodbye and told her she was welcome around the fire anytime as long as there were no more ghost stories.

I suggested we all go to bed as well and when we discovered we all needed to pee, we all walked to the toilet area together with five separate flashlights. Jason brought along the stick he was using to poke the fire, "just in case."

Anna and I finished peeing before the rest. Anna hatched a plan to scare Jason, and I was obviously on board. She took a twig and used it to quietly lock him in by inserting it through the holes where a padlock would go. Then she let out a scream and threw herself against the outside of the stall he was in.

When Jason yelled, "Anna! Anna! Are you ok?"

I yelled back, "Jason, I don't know what happened. I came out of the toilet, and she was on the ground. Help me!"

Jason jiggled the door handle frantically and then, suddenly, came bursting through and landed in a heap on the ground. By now we were all standing together laughing. Let's just say that he was not very happy.

"You, assholes!" he gasped. "I almost had a heart attack. I thought something had seriously happened to Anna. I thought the ghost had come and got you all. I don't know what I thought. You scared me!" As he spoke, he calmed down and then he laughed with us.

We all walked back to our tent, once again marked by a purple glowstick. We said our goodnights and I crawled into my sleeping bag. I was so tired, yet wide awake. I eventually fell asleep.

CHAPTER 9

WE ALL SLEPT in. It was Wednesday, the first day of the festival, and we were all excited. I was first out of my tent, at about seven thirty. I was just getting back from my cold shower — I really needed to get up even earlier or to shower later in the day — when Tia and Dwayne popped out of their tent.

"Did you sleep well?" Dwayne asked me.

"Surprisingly," I responded. "I guess I was really tired. That story didn't even keep me awake. What about you guys?"

"I laid awake for a while, but Tia fell asleep almost instantly. She was in the arms of her big, strong, handsome man, after all." Dwayne smiled. I gave him a punch in the arm and Tia laughed.

"Hey, hey, what's all the noise out here?" Anna said as she crawled out of her tent with Jason right behind her.

"Oh, Beth was just hitting on my man again." Tia ribbed. It was good to see her coming out of her shell. We didn't know her too well since she hadn't grown up in Fredericton as we had. She and Dwayne met when he was shopping at her parents' grocery store, and Tia helped him select a good roast beef for his mom. Dwayne says she flirted with him first, but I think it was the other way around. Either way, they seemed great together.

The four of them excused themselves and headed to the showers and toilets. "Heads up, the water's cold." I called after them.

I got dressed for the day and made sure I had my tickets, credit card, debit card, and ID all in my fanny pack. I always hid them at night; you never know how deeply you'll sleep or who might be in the next tent. The zipper on this one was against my hip and was made of leather "so no one can open it or cut it off you without you knowing," Dad had said. I never told him, but I admired his wisdom. He was so even keeled and trustworthy. He got on my nerves like all parents do, but we knew we loved and respected each other. He was the first one to give me a hug when I told him and Mom that Jason and I broke up. He was the first one to congratulate me when I found out I had gotten into veterinary college, and the first to cheer me on whenever I tried something new. He was also the one who taught me how to drive, hunt, and fish. Dad was the one who bought me my first beer, although I didn't like it much.

There was no need to make coffee or a fire this morning, as we were having breakfast in town. It was likely to be brunch by the time we all got ready. Tonight's concert was Bruno Mars. I couldn't remember who the openers were, but I was looking forward to his music. I only really got to know it when he played the halftime show at the Superbowl. Our church, Greenwood Drive Baptist, had a Superbowl Party and Dad had convinced me to go with him. I wasn't much into football, but I knew the commercials could be fun, and the halftime show was always pretty great. Besides, there promised to be a ton of food. Jason had come with us. I liked the fact that Mars had a complete horn section and played some great music to dance to. He was good-looking, too. I thought it was a great way to start the festival.

We got into town around ten and decided to go to Annie's as they had the bigger menu selection. The guys wanted more than just coffee and pastry, and so did I, quite frankly. I like my meals.

Breakfast was delicious. We all decided to eat a big meal so we wouldn't need lunch. Jason and I both had steak and eggs. My eight-ounce ribeye was cooked a perfect medium. My two eggs were over easy so that I could dip my toast in the runny, golden yolk. And I had the home fries done on the grill without onions. Delicious.

Jason had his steak medium rare and home fries done in the fryer. Anna went with a standard breakfast special: scrambled eggs, toast, home fries (on the grill like mine) and two sausage links. Tia had a western omelette and rye toast while Dwayne carb-loaded with two Belgian waffles covered in fresh strawberries and whipped cream with a side of bacon. Everything tasted as good as it looked.

When our server Kaylin brought our check, I asked, "What can you tell me about the funeral home? I hear there is a ghost."

Kaylin stopped midway to picking up a glass as she cleared the table. Her face twisted a little and then returned to normal a second later. "You don't want to go near there unless you have to. I'd advise you to stay away."

"Why? Is it haunted?" I pressed her.

"That Mr. O'Reagan is a different sort. He and the sheriff always seem to be conspiring about something. A couple years ago the FBI came to town looking for a couple of lost hikers. I think one was the son of someone important. Anyway, the sheriff and Mr. O'Reagan seemed to be meeting every day while they were here. The FBI questioned both of them. It was probably just procedure, but still, it made me wonder. They've been friends since high school, so if something was going on with one of them, you know they'd help each other. As for your ghost, I've heard rumours, but I've never set foot in that funeral home so wouldn't know much about it. Just you remember what I tell you and don't go near that place or Mr. O'Reagan. Nothing good can come of it." With that, she placed our bill on the table, cleared as much as she could carry, and left us sitting there, filled with more questions.

We decided it would be a good time to explore the rest of downtown. As we went up the street, we passed a men's shop, Adam's Attire for Men. There was a mannequin in the window dressed in the latest fashions. Neither of the guys had any interest in going in.

Then we found the barber shop, simply called Barber Shoppe. Next was the office of Dr. Ken Webb, DDS. It appeared he was having a busy day, with a full waiting room. We found the other ladies' store Tia was looking for, Fran's Finery. I wondered if there really was a Fran or if someone was just going for the alliteration. With a little skip in her step, Tia went in, and we filed in behind her.

The shop was brightly lit, but not harshly. It was bigger than I would have guessed from the outside, and full, but tastefully laid out. Jason spotted some seats at the back near the changing rooms and that's where the guys spent the next hour or so, playing on their phones, only looking up when one of us asked, "How do I look in this, boys?" I think we may have set a world record. Tia bought two complete outfits. The first was more casual. It started with a pair of poly-blend capris. They were striped yellow and grey with pinstripes of white. She complimented it with a white top, making the pinstripes pop. She found a pair of yellow canvas sneakers and grey ankle socks. Completing the outfit was a yellow scrunchie for her long brown hair. The whole outfit was adorable and really showed off her dark complexion. I had never noticed just how beautiful she was until now. I was a little jealous.

Her second outfit was a light blue minidress. In a bigger size it might look good on me. She paired it with a soft cream-coloured shawl and matching clutch. For shoes she chose a smart pair of navy flats that matched the buttons going up the front of the dress. Tia was a smart shopper and great at pulling an ensemble together.

I could tell Dwayne liked both outfits as he almost had to pick his jaw up off the floor. When she came out of the dressing room in her original outfit he stood up and gave her a kiss. "You could easily be a model, babe," he said.

Anna found a great pair of jeans that really showed off her curves. Not too tight, but they fit her snuggly in all the right places. There were little flowers embroidered at the slightly flared cuffs. She chose a simple, muted yellow, cold shoulder top with embroidered flowers on the front. When Jason saw her, he whistled and then laughed when she did a little spin.

While I didn't have anyone special to impress, I joined the fashionista show. I tried on several different outfits and bought my favourite. It was a pretty little A-line dress with a V-neck that flared out from my waste with its box pleats and stopped just above my knees. The spaghetti strap bodice hugged my toned body and accentuated my breasts. The luxe satin reminded me of a prom dress. When I came out of the dressing room and did a twirl, I felt like a princess. It felt good to see Jason take a second look. *Sorry dude, can't touch this!* I thought with a smile.

We left Fran's, crossed an intersection, and came to the supermarket. I wondered if the produce was all from Bel's father's farm. Then we were at the edge of the town square, but not before we came to a little ice cream shop, Summer Sweets. By the name, I assumed it was a seasonal shop. We each got an ice cream cone and then we crossed to the little park to eat by the fountain. We people-watched for a bit. There were a lot of people to watch. That's when I spotted the tall man again. I now knew his name was Conor.

He looked around and spotted me looking his direction. He smiled and waved and then headed inside. I involuntarily shuddered, but chalked it up to a cold ice cream on a hot day.

Dwayne saw me looking at the funeral home. "Are you looking for the ghost?"

I laughed, "No."

"I think it would be fun to spend the night in the funeral home and see if the ghost comes out," Jason said.

'No!" exclaimed Tia. "Are you crazy? There is no circumstance that would cause me to do that. I'm not spending the *night* in a funeral home, let alone a haunted one. Remember what Kaylin told us? Stay away!"

We all laughed, except Jason. I thought he was serious, but I just shrugged it off. I didn't see any way he could convince everyone to break into a funeral home at night to see a ghost. I shuddered again.

I noticed a young couple sitting on the edge of the fountain. It was clear they liked each other and that it was a new relationship. Both appeared nervous and the conversation seemed a little halting, forced. The was some nervous laughter, some holding of hands and then I watched as he leaned in and kissed her. She returned the kiss.

We walked back to the car. Tia led the way. She was still a little put out that Jason had suggested breaking in to O'Reagan's. I thought it was funny that she was so much in a huff over something so small. She was scared, like me, and trying not to show it.

When we got back the car Jason said, "I'm sorry if I upset you, Tia. I didn't mean to. I just thought it would be cool to stake out the place and see if the stories were true. If you're too scared, I won't mention it again."

I thought this was a bit of an unnecessary dig and was a little surprised at him.

"I'm not scared," responded Tia. "I just think it's a stupid idea. If we got caught, we could end up in jail, and I'm not going to jail for some half-baked plan to see if there is a ghost in a funeral home." With that, she got in the car, in the back seat where I normally sat. I climbed in beside her, leaving Dwayne alone in the middle row, with Jason and Anna once again in the front.

As we drove back to the farm, I saw Anna lean over and say something to Jason. He looked in the rear-view mirror at Tia, shook his head, and kept driving. Anna turned and smiled at us and then turned her attention back to the front.

"Are you ok?" I asked Tia.

"I'm fine," she said. "Just a little creeped out. I don't like the idea of ghosts *or* funeral homes, let alone the two of them together. I remember when my grandmother died. My family got a call that she wasn't doing well, a call we had received several times over the previous couple of weeks. I decided to stay home, and then the phone rang again a few minutes later. It was the special care home again. They told me my grandmother had just passed on. I got in my car and met my parents there. I couldn't bring myself to kiss her or hold her hand, so instead I stood at the end of the bed. I said my goodbyes from there, and reached out and grabbed her foot and told her I loved her. The next night I woke up in the middle of the night and saw my grandmother at the foot of my bed. She was just standing there. When I called her name, she smiled. She reached out, grabbed my foot and said, 'I love you too, dear,' and then she disappeared. I didn't know if I was dreaming, or if it was actually her, or her spirit, at least. I told my parents the next day. My dad didn't believe me and suggested that I should seek counselling to help deal with my grief. Later, my mom talked to me and said that she believed me. She said that I was lucky as it meant my grandmother truly loved me, and that she was concerned about me. Concerned enough that she needed to be sure I was okay, and that I knew she loved me. She said that it meant I had a special gift, a connection with the afterlife, and that I could speak with the dead. Over the years I've seen a number of spirits, or ghosts, but I've just ignored them. I don't want to believe it, so I've never talked about it. I've brushed them off as my imagination. So, when Jason suggested we actually seek out a ghost, I got defensive."

"Tia," I said, "Oh wow! That's quite an experience. If it helps, I believe you did see your grandmother. I think that sometimes, God, or whoever, allows those we love to come back to help us get closure. I don't think that ever happens to harm us, though. And I don't believe we need to fear those who come back. Even if there is a ghost at the funeral home, I think it would be cool to say hello and even help them if they need something."

I didn't realize it, but Dwayne was listening. He turned. "Babe, why didn't you tell me that before?" he asked Tia. "I'm sorry if I was insensitive. I love you, Tia." He reached his hand back and took hers in his. They stayed that way for the rest of the ride.

Back at the campground there was quite a commotion. Sheriff Johnston was there with three other police officers, two male and one female. The lights on the top of the two police cars were on, and a crowd had gathered.

We stopped just inside the makeshift gate, and I asked the first person I saw, a young brunette woman, and found out that someone had gone missing. Someone had called the police to report that their friend hadn't come back the night before. The last time they'd seen him was near the fountain just before midnight. He had connected with a girl and had wanted to spend time with her. He'd told his friends he would walk back to the campground.

"I wonder if it was that couple we saw at the fountain?" I exclaimed. "We should check and see."

I didn't wait for a response and hurried to where Sheriff Johnson and his deputies were standing.

"Excuse me," I said. "Who are you looking for?"

"We're looking for Andrew Buck," one of the deputies said.

"Is he about six feet tall with light brown hair?" I inquired. "If so, I think I saw him last night."

The sheriff was called, and I told him about seeing the couple sitting by the fountain and then walking off together, up the road past the funeral home and towards the residential area. He thanked me and said it would be helpful in their search.

I rejoined the group, and we headed back to our tents. *I hope they find him*, I thought.

CHAPTER 10

BY THREE O'CLOCK we were all ready to go. I double checked my fanny pack to ensure I had enough cash for some festival food, and a T-shirt if I saw one I liked, as well as a little extra for any emergencies. I brought a light jacket in case it got chilly later. I was dressed in my favourite pair of side-slit boot-cut jeans (I don't usually care about the latest fashions, but I really liked these), with my New Balance 997s so that I would be able to stand all evening without hurting my feet. After all, I needed to stand for four days in a row. And I put on the blue top that I'd bought the day before. I was ready for a fun night filled with music and friends.

We pulled out of the farm at ten past three and headed for the festival. The first bus wouldn't leave until four, the same time the gates opened, so we would beat the majority of the local crowd. We assumed those coming in from Millinocket and other parts of Maine would show up later.

We didn't notice the number of people walking around downtown on the way to the festival grounds. We were all anxious to get there and establish our ground space. If we had paid attention, we would have seen that there were far more of them than the day before. It was a shock, when we pulled up, to find the parking lot almost full and to see hundreds of people already in line. The gates wouldn't even open for a half hour. I was glad we'd decided to come when we did.

"Holy crap!" Jason said when he saw the line. "I guess we should have come an hour ago. We won't make that mistake tomorrow."

We piled out of the car, making sure it was locked up tight behind us. We did note that there were several security personnel walking among the vehicles parked in the makeshift parking lot. I appreciated knowing that someone was watching our car.

"We should get in the line that goes in closest to the sound operator." Dwayne suggested. "That way, when we get in, we have the fastest route to where we want to sit." We all agreed and got in the line.

At the gate, security personnel were checking people with a metal detection wand for weapons, opening purses — only small purses were allowed — and asking about drugs. "Prescription or over-the-counter drugs only," I heard one say.

The line was moving pretty well but then suddenly stopped. A short distance in front of us, a guy was trying to get through the gate with a backpack, which was strictly prohibited. The guy, who I guessed was about thirty, older than us, was really getting animated. Several security personnel had come closer in case the situation escalated.

The security guard, a younger woman about my age, was doing a great job of keeping her cool, despite the guy's continued efforts to push past her.

"Get out of my way!" I heard him yell as he attempted to push her. She shoved him backward, catching him off guard, and he stumbled. Five or six other security people moved in quickly but couldn't deter the idiot, who continued to insist he be allowed to enter with his backpack. Several of the others in line began to yell at him.

"Take the backpack to your car!"

"What don't you understand about no backpacks allowed!"

"Take him down and let the rest of us in!"

The jeers provoked him further and he tried to make a break for it. The original guard, the young woman, stepped in front of him. As he moved to go around, she grabbed the backpack from his hand with one arm, stuck out a foot, and shoved him with the other arm. In one swift move, she had put him on the ground. Face first in the dirt. I let out a little "YES!" under my breath with a fist pump. Anna and Tia both turned my way with a laugh.

The guy jumped up in a flash with a knife in his hand. He was now just on the other side of the chain-link fence. The backpack was on the ground as he turned to face the security guards. I hadn't even seen them coming, but suddenly a dozen or more had him surrounded. He feigned a few strikes at them, but they were careful to maintain a safe distance. I could see they were well trained.

Sheriff Johnson suddenly appeared, stepped into the ring, and said something softly to the armed man, who then just let the knife drop to the ground. The sheriff placed the man's hands behind his back and cuffed him. The crowd cheered as he and his backpack were walked back through the gate and placed into a waiting police car.

It was clear the man feared Johnson, as it had taken him only a couple of words to end the threat.

With the excitement over, the line started to move once again. The whole thing had taken less than ten minutes.

As we went through the gate, Dwayne said, "Well done, Sheriff. I'm impressed."

"Glad to have you protecting us," Tia congratulated.

Johnson nodded. "Thank you. It's what I'm here for."

We walked past the gate and headed for the sound engineers' booth. "Did you see the way that chick took down that guy?" Jason asked us, like we could have missed it. Anna cleared her throat, and Jason said, "I mean, did you see the way that talented young woman took down that guy?" We all laughed.

"She was amazing," Tia responded. "I've been taking Tai Kwan Do and hope to someday have reflexes like that."

"You better watch out Dwayne," I teased, "or Tia might put you down like that."

"Anytime she wants," smiled Dwayne. Tia blushed.

We ended up a little closer to the stage than we had anticipated. I didn't mind, as now we could see the performers a little better.

We had just laid out our blankets when Tia asked Anna and me, "Do you want to go check out the merch tables? If we go now, we will have our choice."

We went to the back of the festival grounds and scoped out the tables. We didn't have to wait long to get to the front of the line as most people were still filing in. Not surprisingly, merchandise was expensive, especially considering the exchange rate. I bought a great Taylor Swift tour sweatshirt for forty dollars. It listed all the tour stops on the back and had an artistic picture of Taylor on the front. Anna didn't get anything for herself, but she did buy a shirt for Jason, "since he has such a crush on Miss Swift." That left Tia. I knew her parents had some money, but I never dreamed she would be able to spend so much. She bought an autographed picture of each of the three bands we were seeing that night. She bought herself a sweatshirt — now I knew why she hadn't brought a jacket. She also bought some glow sticks and other knick-knacks. She spent almost two hundred dollars altogether.

We stopped at one of the stations giving away water. We took ten bottles in case they ran out later in the evening. I didn't want to be left drinking soda all night. I enjoyed a Coke every now and then but preferred to drink water most of the time.

It took us about an hour to get back to Dwayne and Jason, who were tossing a frisbee back and forth with a couple of other guys. "We thought maybe you weren't coming back," greeted Dwayne. "I'm glad you did."

They introduced us to their new friends, Adam and Andy. They were a couple from New Hampshire and were staying in Millinocket. They said the drive in had been crazy, and that the next time, they would camp here in town.

The guys played for a little while longer before joining us on the blankets. There was still an hour until concert time, and I decided to close my eyes for a bit.

CHAPTER 11

I MUST HAVE DOZED off. Anna was shaking my shoulders, "Wake up, lazy bones. The concert is going to start soon." I looked at my watch and saw that it was ten to seven.

The first to take the stage was the local group, The Ghost of Paul Revere. The morning host of a local radio station, Steve something-or-other, came out on stage and welcomed everyone to the festival. He told us the band was an award-winning folk group "from right here in Maine!" Everyone cheered. He asked us all to give them a warm welcome and we all cheered again as they struck the first chord.

The band featured lots of facial hair. The lead singer was a big guy with a long beard. He played guitar. Another guy played the banjo and sang and a third played the bass and sang. I didn't catch their names as they spoke with a bit of a twang. They sang for about thirty minutes and told us all that they were releasing a new album in the fall titled *Good at Losing Everything*. I looked at Jason and thought, "Yup. I know all about that!" The band was pretty good, just too twangy for my style.

After The Ghost finished, Tia asked if anyone was hungry, and I realized I was. I remembered I hadn't eaten since brunch. Tia and I offered to go get snacks from the line of the food trucks across the back of the site. There was everything from burgers and dogs to fish and chips and assorted carnival foods. After we had everyone's order, Tia and I went off to get dinner.

"So, Dwyane tells me that you and Jason used to date."

"Yeah," I said. "We started dating in middle school and dated all through high school. We met at Park Street Elementary and were friends almost from the first day we met. He finally got up the nerve to tell me he liked me in grade seven, and we dated from then on. We even talked about getting married after high school, but it didn't work out. We broke up in the summer after grade twelve. He and Anna started dating about a year ago."

"That must be more than a little awkward," Tia responded.

"It is," I replied. "Anna's my best friend, but we've kind of grown apart since they got together. We used to be glued at the hip, even when Jason and I were together. Anna was always with us, or we would often have girl's nights. When she and Jason got together, I just couldn't hang out with them that much, you know? It hurt that he had moved on, especially with my best friend. I'm working on not letting it bother me, but I still have my moments."

"I'm sorry to hear that. Can I ask why you guys broke up? I don't mean to pry, just hoping to get to know you better." Tia asked.

"I don't really want to talk about it," I said. "I haven't told anyone, not Anna or even my parents. It was actually Jason that left me, not the other way around. It's as much Jason's story as mine, and I don't want to hurt his reputation or cause any trouble with him and Anna. So, I've kept quiet. I'm pretty sure he didn't tell Anna either. I think the only people who know the whole story are his parents. They don't talk to me anymore."

Thankfully, we arrived at the food trucks, so she didn't ask for more details.

I got the fish and chips from one truck while Tia got Dwayne's pizza. Tia and I both wanted a souvlaki plate, so we met in line at the Dimitri's truck.

"So, what about you, Tia? You've been dating Dwayne for what, nine months now?" I inquired.

"Eleven," she said.

"When did you move to Fredericton and where from? And how did you meet?"

"Well let's see. We moved to Fredericton just over a year ago from Tobique First Nation where my parents owned a convenience store and gas bar. The Chief at St. Mary's reached out and asked if they would come and run their supermarket. Mom and Dad jumped at the chance, and we moved as soon as school was out, two months later. They wanted to let me finish grade eleven at Nackawic Senior High, and then I graduated last month from FHS.

"I met Dwayne one day when he came into the store. I was putting hamburger in the display case filling the display case with hamburger and he asked me for some advice on a good roast. I offered to package one just for him and when I did, he was very thankful. He asked if he could by me a coffee when I got off. I thought he was really cute and very nice, so I said yes. We met at the Tim Horton's down the street, and I had a blast talking to him. He asked me to a movie, *Jurassic World, Fallen Kingdom*, and we've been together ever since. My parents were a little, um, cautious about his age. Not that four years is a lot, but I was only 17 then, and he was 21. He's such a gentleman." Tia's face glowed as she talked about him.

"Well, I'm glad he met you," I replied. "And I'm happy we got to this spend time alone together."

"I'm happy too." She replied.

Once we had all the food in our hands, we headed back.

"I think you should tell Anna about whatever happened between you and Jason," she suddenly blurted. "I'm sorry, I should mind my own business," she quickly added.

"That's ok. But I think Jason is the one who should tell her. Or maybe Anna should ask." I responded.

"Maybe I'll tell her to." Tia said. "I think she feels a little lost between the two of you, not knowing. She didn't say anything, but I can sense she's torn now that she and Jason are dating."

We didn't have time for any more talk as we arrived back at our little patch of ground. We handed out the food to a chorus of thanks and sat to eat just as the MC returned to the stage. Most of the crowd stood once again, but we remained seated to eat. We didn't know much about The Dianas, other than that they were a girl's group from Australia. They weren't bad but definitely not my style. Tia seemed to like them, though. She got up and danced away for a bit.

When they finished, there was a short break to reset the stage, and the sound engineers checked the various speakers and mics. The lighting technicians made sure their presets were working properly, and the pyrotechnics staff checked their riggings. I'd heard that Bruno put on a terrific concert, and I hoped the hype was right. As we waited, Anna and Tia went to get us some sodas. Shortly after they returned, the

MC picked up the mic and once again welcomed us to the festival.

"Folks, I have a very important announcement to make. Can you please direct your attention to the screens." The screens showed pictures of the missing couple. Their names were below their pictures, Jason Thatcher and Jill Currie. "Last night two of our own went missing. If anyone has information of their whereabouts, please go to one of the medical tents and report what you know. A uniformed officer will be there to take any statements. Once again, please, if you know anything, go to a medical tent and make a statement. Let's all pray for their safe return."

After a small pause he spoke again. "Bruno Mars was born in Hawaii. In 2003, he moved to Los Angeles to pursue a career in music. After writing songs for other artists including "Nothin' on You" by B.o.B. and "Billionaire" by Travie McCoy, he released his first album, *Doo-Wops & Hooligans*, in 2010, spawning international number one singles "Just the Way You Are," "Grenade," and "The Lazy Song." In 2012, he released his second album *Unorthodox Jukebox*, which was his first number one on the Billboard 200. Two songs from that album, "Locked Out of Heaven" and "When I Was Your Man" climbed the billboard charts all the way to number one. His third album, *24K Magic*, received seven Grammy Awards. Please give a warm Maine welcome to Bruno Mars!"

The band began to play, and Bruno emerged from the back of the stage to thunderous applause. The beat set in and he began to sing "24K Magic." When he finished, he addressed the audience, thanking us all for coming, and joking that he hoped we didn't have early curfews.

The concert lasted almost two hours. He played just about every song I knew. I danced and sang along with him and the crowd. The pyrotechnics were tasteful, and the sound was impeccable. He was joined on stage by dancers and backup vocalists throughout the evening.

It was after midnight by the time we got back to the car.

"That was awesome!" Tia exclaimed. "I didn't know a lot of Bruno's songs before, but he is so amazing."

"I had such a great time, guys," I said. "Thanks for bringing me along as the fifth wheel."

"No fifth wheel here!" Tia responded. "I've loved having you along on the trip. I can't imagine it without you."

"Same here," responded Anna. "We haven't spent nearly enough time together lately. I've missed my best friend."

Jason shot me a glance that only Tia seemed to notice.

Traffic was heavier than we expected on the way back, but we beat the first bus load. We all made a beeline for the showers. Our plan was to shower at night so that we would miss the lines and the freezing cold water in the morning.

When I got back the tent site, once again lit by a purple glow stick, I found Tia and Anna sitting around the fire, talking. "You were fast," I remarked. "Where are the guys?"

"They haven't made it back yet." Anna responded.

"You looked deep in conversation when I walked up. I hope I didn't interrupt anything important," I said.

"Nah, we were just talking about the boys," smiled Tia. "Nothing important."

Just then the guys walked up.

"I think I'm going to head to bed. I'm really tired and I want to go for a walk before breakfast. Does anyone want to join me?" I had no takers on the walk, but everyone wished me good night.

I could hear them talking around the fire, but they were quiet so I couldn't make out what they were saying. I soon drifted off to sleep.

CHAPTER 12

I WOKE UP TO Anna's voice. "Beth. Pssst, Beth, are you awake? Beth?"

"Hello?" I responded. What's wrong?"

"Can I come in? I need to talk."

"What? Uh, sure. Come on in," I said groggily as I sat up.

"I'm not sure where to start," began Anna. "Jason and I just had a fight. Well, a talk really, and I got upset and needed to come see you. I hope that's ok."

"A fight? What about? Are you ok?" My mind raced to wake up.

Anna sighed and lay down, using my backpack as a pillow. "So," she began. After a big pause she continued, "Jason and I just had a big talk." Another pause. "About what happened between the two of you. Why didn't you tell me?"

I stayed silent.

"He told me about prom night and then he went on to tell me that you thought you were pregnant. The short version is that he was scared to death and went to his parents, who were furious. There was a lot of yelling about how he had ruined his life. Apparently, they called you a few choice names and forbid him to see you again. When he refused, they took his phone and bought a plane ticket. They drove him to the airport and sent him to his cousins' in Toronto for two weeks. Jason said he didn't even get to pack his own clothes. When he got there, he learned his parents had made his aunt and uncle promise that he wouldn't be given access to the internet. He was forbidden to even use the phone. They kept him busy, taking him all over. They went to a Jays game, to Niagara Falls, toured wine country. He even spent a week in Muskoka at the cottage of one of their friends. The cottage didn't have a phone or internet. Just satellite TV and the lake.

When he got back, you were so mad you wouldn't even talk to him. You wouldn't even give him a chance to apologize. He said it wasn't your fault. That he should have found a way, and that he was ashamed he hadn't done more. I told him he sure should have. I got mad at him for treating you so badly and for not telling me. Why didn't you ever tell me, Beth? I thought we were best friends."

I sat in silence for a few minutes. This was a lot to absorb in the middle of the night. It was like a scene in a soap opera.

Finally, I responded. "You're right," I said. "I should have told you. I was just so embarrassed. I thought Jason and I would get married. We'd even been talking about it. Then, when I thought I was pregnant, he just took off. He didn't answer my texts and emails. His parents wouldn't talk to me, other than to say he was in Toronto visiting his cousins. When I realized I wasn't pregnant, it was too late. I was furious at Jason. We'd already broken up." The tears were flowing now, and I had to catch my breath. "I didn't know how to tell you. I was scared the pregnancy thing would get back to my folks, and you know how they are." Anna was in tears now, too. "I was humiliated that Jason would leave me so fast at the first sign of trouble. I didn't know what to do. So, I did nothing. Anna, you weren't the only one I didn't tell. I never told my parents, or my sister. I didn't tell anyone at all. But I was so angry as well. Angry at myself for having sex with a guy who just took off on me — I gave him my virginity! Angry at Jason for leaving. Angry at everything. By the time I stopped being angry, I was tired. And then I just wanted to put it behind me. When you started dating Jason, I didn't know what to do. I thought about telling you, but I didn't want you to think I was just jealous. I didn't want to hurt you, or Jason. I figured he would tell you when you guys started dating. The longer you dated, the more I was sure he must have told you, and that you were okay with it. I've tried to still feel like best friends, but it's been so hard.

I'm sorry, Anna. I should have told you."

We were both bawling by now. We must have cried for ten minutes before Anna found the words: "I forgive you Beth. I'm sorry I wasn't there for you. I'm sorry I didn't push you more to tell me. I could have been a better friend."

"Me too," I cried, and then we were both bawling again. She sat up and we hugged.

I'm not sure how long we stayed in the tent talking and crying, but we both eventually fell asleep. When I woke up, Anna was snoring, so I quietly slipped from the tent. Tia was by the fire.

"Are you ok?" she asked. "I wasn't eavesdropping, I promise, but it was hard not to hear you guys talking and crying."

"We're fine," I replied. "We had a good talk. One that was long overdue. Did you have anything to do with it?"

"I hope you don't mind, but I did tell Anna that she might want to ask why you and Jason had broken up. It just seemed like you both needed to have a conversation about it. I'm sorry if I overstepped."

"Part of me is mad that you said anything," I told her, "but I owe you a thank you. If you hadn't said anything, we might never have talked about it. At least Anna knows what happened now. Maybe it will help us become best friends again, and not just in name." I looked around and for the first time noticed that we were alone. "Where are they guys?" I asked.

"Dwayne suggested he and Jason go for a walk to give us girls a chance to talk and get breakfast ready. They should be back in a little while." Tia told me.

"Good morning," Anna greeted as she climbed out of the tent. She stretched and gave a big yawn. "Next time I sleep in your tent, Beth, you better have a second camp mattress. I am so stiff this morning."

"I'm so glad you came to talk, Anna, even though it meant waking me up from a great dream about Chris Hemsworth. Next time, though, maybe we can get a good night's sleep first? I am way too tired this morning." I smiled. Anna smiled back.

"Sure thing," she said. "And the next time I consider dating one of your ex-boyfriends, I'll be sure to push you for info first." The two of us hugged.

Anna turned to Tia, "And thank you for suggesting I talk to Jason. I realize we don't know each other very well, but if you hadn't spoken up, we would all still be on eggshells around each other. Now, there may be a few hard feelings to work through, but at least everything is out in the open."

"Yes, thank you, Tia. I can see why Dwayne likes you so much. You have a great head on your shoulders," I said. Then we were all hugging each other.

We turned our attention to making breakfast. I pulled out some Aunt Jemima pancake mix and added in some water. Half regular spring water and half sparkling water. Dad had taught me that if I added some sparkling water, it made fluffier pancakes. Anna set herself to the task of making scrambled eggs, and Tia made toast and coffee.

Just as I pulled the last of the pancakes off the skillet, the boys showed up. Jason always did have a knack for appearing right when food was ready. My mom used to set an extra place at the dinner table just in case he showed up. He did, often. I suddenly flashed to Jason and me and my parents laughing and eating dinner together. I missed it.

Anna was first to greet them. "Hi, Dwayne. Hey, Jason." I noted that she greeted Dwayne first, and that there were some undertones in the way she said "Jason." I could tell that they still had some things to work out between them, and likely with me, too. But at least we all knew the truth.

CHAPTER 13

THERE WASN'T MUCH conversation at breakfast. Tia and Dwayne felt the tension and kept pretty much to themselves. As we finished, I looked at Jason and took a deep breath. "Can we go for a walk?" I asked him. Jason turned and looked at Anna who gave a slight nod.

"Sure," he said. "I guess we need to talk."

Tia piped in with, "Dwayne and I will clean up so you two can walk." She turned to Anna. "Do you want to help?" I realized I was still in my pyjamas. I didn't even have makeup on, and my eyes were probably still puffy from crying last night and again this morning. Suddenly, I was really aware of my appearance. I slipped quickly into my tent, put on a clean T-shirt, and ran a comb through my hair. I couldn't do anything about the puffy eyes, but I did put on a little mascara.

When I emerged from my tent, Jason was standing with Dwayne, talking. Tia had gathered the dishes and had started to wash them in the tub. I assumed Anna was changing.

Jason looked over and, seeing me, walked over. "Hey," he said.

I responded likewise. "Hey."

There was an awkward minute before he started walking. He turned and asked, "Are you coming? I guess we need to talk . . . ." He paused, then said, "Finally."

Finally. That stung a little. I guess I deserved it. Eventually it had gotten easy for us to just not be alone together. Childish, I know. But easier than talking about it.

I sighed and followed Jason, winding through the tents. I distracted myself by taking notice of all the different styles and tent colours. There were red single-person tents and yellow three-person ones. Someone had even brought along a gigantic blue one that must have slept ten and still had room for luggage. There were even a few tent trailers in the mix — now that was a great idea! Maybe next time we could bring one of those.

When we got to the road, Jason stopped. "I'm sorry, Beth," he said. "I'm sorry I left. I'm sorry I failed you. I'm sorry I didn't try harder to connect. I'm sorry I didn't push harder to get you to talk when I got back. I'm sorry I didn't stand up to my parents. I'm sorry I hurt you like that. Most of all though, I'm sorry I ruined our relationship. I did love you Beth, but . . . ," he trailed off and sighed.

That's when I first looked at him. He had tears in his eyes. His posture wasn't what I was used to. Jason was normally so strong looking, with great posture. He was so confident and sure of himself. Right now, though, he was hunched over, quiet, insecure. His head hung like he was a bad dog I'd just scolded.

I reached out and took both his hands. "I forgive you. I'm still hurt and mad and frustrated and sad and a whole bunch of other feelings that I don't understand, but I forgive you." I paused to consider my next words. "Jason, I'm sorry too. I'm sorry I never gave you a chance to explain, to talk. If I had, maybe we could have salvaged our relationship. Maybe things would have been different. I don't know what might have been, but I should have given you a chance. I was just so hurt. I felt betrayed too." By now we were both in tears. I let go of his hands and wiped my eyes with the back of my hand, drying it on my jeans. Jason ducked his head and used the sleeve of his T-shirt to do the same.

I sighed, turned, and began to walk towards the lake. After a couple of steps Jason was at my side. "So, what really happened?" I asked. "I mean, Anna told me some stuff last night, but I think I'd like to finally hear it from you. She's really pissed at you, by the way."

After a moment, Jason began his story. "When you told me you thought you were pregnant, I freaked. I didn't know what to do. We were so young. I wasn't ready to be a dad. I was so immature. I knew that I loved you, and that we had talked about getting married, but it was way too soon.

"The day after you told me, my parents forced it out of me. They could tell something was wrong. I didn't eat dinner or watch TV. I just went to my room and stayed there. Dad threatened to break down the door if I didn't unlock it. They came in, and Mom sat on the edge of my bed, Dad sat in my desk chair, and they just sat there. They didn't say anything. They just waited.

After I guess about fifteen minutes, I told them. I told them we had spent the night together. That we had slept together. I told them that you had called and told me you thought you were pregnant. That you had missed your period. At first, they were just quiet. Then Mom said, 'That little hussy isn't going to ruin your life. Your father and I will see to that.' I couldn't believe it. I thought she loved you like a daughter, but she was so mad. 'Bill,' she said, 'What are we going to do? He's too young to get married or have a child. He's just a baby! We have to protect him. I can't believe she would do this to you, Jason. Who does she think she is?' And then she called you a few names. I tried to speak, but she just put up a hand and told me to keep my mouth shut, and that I'd done enough already."

I was crying again. I thought his mom had loved me. She'd always treated me so well. It hurt to hear that she'd talked about me like that. We had come to the edge of the lake, not far from where Bel had taken me fishing. I sat on a fallen tree and patted a spot next to me. Jason sat down and continued.

"Mom went on for a while and then Dad interrupted saying we should all calm down and figure it out. He was so calm, but I could tell he was thinking and was close to a plan. Mom gave him a nasty look but kept quiet. Dad went on to tell me that I made a big mistake, that they liked you, but not the trouble you helped get me into. He asked me if I thought I was ready to be a father. I admitted that I didn't and that I didn't know what to do. We talked about asking you to get an abortion. Mom actually asked if I knew I was really the father. Of course, I knew I was.

"That's when their plan unfolded. They told me that they were sending me out of town for a couple of weeks. I could go spend time with Mom's brother, Ben. They took my phone and my iPad and told me not to call you. Mom went online and bought a plane ticket for a flight the next morning. It was really expensive, over a thousand dollars. I told them I needed to tell you, but they wouldn't let me. Dad actually spent the night in the living room 'so you don't do anything stupid.'

"They drove me to the airport at six the next morning. Uncle Ben and my cousins met me at Pearson Airport and took me to their house. I could tell they were a little uncomfortable, but they didn't say much more than 'hello.' I spent two weeks with them, making small talk. I had no access to a phone or internet. I did tell them what happened so they didn't think I was running from a gang or something. They were really good about the situation and took me to a Jays game and toured me around Niagara Falls. When two weeks were up, they put me back on a plane and I came home.

"When I got home, my parents met me at the airport and took me to dinner at Boston Pizza. We talked, and they told me you had been calling and calling. They also told me that one of the messages you left said that you weren't pregnant. I was relieved to hear it and wanted to call you back, but my parents forbade it for the first few days.

"Finally, a few days later, and after many discussions about sex and protection and my future, I was allowed to reach out, but you wouldn't talk to me. You know I tried. I left voice mails and sent you texts and emails, but you never returned them. I wanted to apologize and tell you what happened, why I couldn't call."

"I'm sorry," I whispered. "I didn't know."

I was sobbing again. I was so tired. The emotional toll this conversation took, along with the one with Anna the night before, had completely drained me. "I thought so many bad things about you. I thought you were just another one of those guys that ran at the first sign of trouble. I thought you were ghosting me. That you didn't really love me and took off rather than face any trouble. I blamed you. I had no idea it was your parents. I'm sorry. I should have talked to you when you got back, but I was already too hurt and angry, I just couldn't. And then time went on, and it felt like we didn't need to talk. I thought I had gotten over it until you and Anna started dating. I thought about telling her then, but I didn't. I thought you would. I guess I was wrong about that. And now, here we are. All messed up."

We sat there on the log for a while, looking out at the lake. Every once in a while, I saw a fish jump. The lake was so peaceful. The water was like glass. Every fly that landed on the water left its mark of little circles, spreading out until they ran out of steam and just faded away. Across the lake I could see a couple of men fishing. They caught four or five while we sat there in silence. Thinking. Reflecting. Wondering what could have been. I watched some children playing in the water off to our right. There was a small beach where their parents sat on the shore, watching. I watched the few clouds in the bright summer sky float slowly by. One looked like a cross. Another looked like a dog. Still another looked like an angel with its wings spread out to fly.

I don't know how long we sat there before Jason spoke. "What now?" The question was both simple and complicated.

"I don't know," I responded, "I guess we just figure it out along the way. I think we just need time now that everything is all out in the open. Let's just take it one step at a time. Jason, I still love you, just not in *that* way anymore. I think you and Anna need some time to figure things out too. She was pretty pissed last night when she came to my tent."

"I guess you're right," Jason said. "We better get back. It'll be time to go to the concert soon if we want a good spot again."

We stood up. Jason stooped down, picked up a stone, and skipped it across the surface of the water, and then we went back to the campground. I was so tired.

CHAPTER 14

ANNA, TIA, AND Dwayne were sitting around the campfire, talking. We had been gone longer than I'd thought. It was almost noon. Gates would open in a few minutes for today's concert. I didn't care about the opening acts that would play that afternoon. I just wanted to hear Ed Sheeran that evening.

"I think I need to have a nap. Why don't you guys go this afternoon, grab a spot, and then I can join you later? I'll just take the bus over."

"Actually, we talked about it," Tia said, "and we all felt like we should just skip the afternoon concerts and take the bus over together in time to see Ed." Everyone nodded in agreement.

"It's settled then," declared Dwayne. "We're all going to relax this afternoon before seeing the big concert. In the meantime, Tia and I are going to run into town and get some hamburger so we can make lunch. It will save us some money too, by not buying another meal from the food trucks."

"I think I'll go for walk," I said. I ducked into my tent to grab some extra bug spray and my sunhat and headed off. I needed a little "me time."

I was thankful to be alone. I wandered along the lakeshore and stopped by the water's edge. The water was as flat as a mirror. I picked up a stone and skipped it across the water. Five skips. I spent the next half hour trying to increase my skip count. When I got to fifteen countable skips, I sat down to stare out at the water and think.

I thought back to my conversations with Jason and Anna. To everything that had happened, then and since. To the damage that had been done to my friendships with them. The time that had been wasted. I could feel some of the tension leave my body as I began to cry. I cried tears of release. I shuddered, sobbing. I cried like I'd never cried before. And the heaviness I'd felt for so long rolled away.

Finally, I felt able to be honest with my friends, and with myself.

As I got back to the edge of the farm, I ran into Bel. I welcomed the distraction.

"Hey, Bel. How are you?" I asked.

"I'm good," she replied. "I just finished my chores and was heading to the lake for a swim. Are you up for joining me or are you heading to the concert?"

"I just had a shower, so I'm not up for a swim, but when you're done, why don't you swing by my tent? We can have a visit," I invited.

"Sounds good. I'll see you in about an hour."

I weaved my way back to camp without giving another thought to the events of the last twelve hours. Well, I tried not to give it a thought.

I arrived back at camp to the delicious scent of burgers, onions, and mushrooms grilling over a fire of maple wood. The smell reminded me of a Louisiana Bar and Grill I'd eaten at when I'd flown down to visit a state-of-the-art vet clinic while I was in school: they'd cooked everything over an open flame using only maple wood. I started to salivate like one of Pavlov's dogs. I was hungry.

The burgers were delicious. I ate two. When we were finished, Tia asked, "Did you guys notice an ice cream truck is now parked on the road by the entrance? I saw a few people going by with cones while you were off for your walk. Does anyone want to come with me for some dessert?"

Everyone thought that was a good idea. I piped up, "It's ladies' treat. We'll go and get cones for everyone. What'll it be, guys?" Jason ordered his typical chocolate and Dwayne asked for strawberry. We skipped off together.

The mood had really lightened. When we arrived at the truck, there was a long line of about thirty ahead of us.

On the side of the truck, beside the list of ice cream flavours, was a poster with a picture of the couple who had gone missing, asking anyone who had seen them to contact the local authorities. The prevailing thought was that they'd got lost in the woods. A common occurrence out here, apparently.

Back at the tents, the guys were busy talking with Bel. I had forgotten about her!

"Hi Bel!" we all greeted in perfect unison. We looked at each other and giggled. Tia and Anna each handed cones to their guys.

"Hi girls," smiled Bel. "You all seem to be in a good mood today!"

"We have ice cream," I said. "What could be better?

"You guys seemed to be in a deep discussion about something," Anna remarked. "What were you talking about?"

"Ghosts," Jason said.

"Yeah, we were asking Bel more about the ghost that haunts the funeral home. We were hoping maybe there were even more." Dwayne was excited. I didn't know he was so into ghost stories.

"Not this again!" exclaimed Tia. "I told you I'm not interested."

"Relax," Dwayne told her. "We were just asking if she knew anything else. I'd still like to see him for myself though." Tia simply rolled her eyes in response.

"Well, what did you learn?" I asked, suddenly interested. "Is there just the one, or is the old ghost town haunted too?"

"As far as I know, it's just the one," Bel responded. "I've never actually been inside the funeral home. But I do believe I've seen the little boy," she continued. "I go to town early every other morning to take fresh eggs or produce to the market. I usually park in the town square and walk through town, towing a wagon of food behind me. On a couple of occasions, I swear I saw him in one of the windows, but when I looked back, he was always gone. Then, one morning I know I saw him because he spoke to me. I was loading up the cart, and when I turned from the truck with a big box of vegetables, I caught the edge of the side rail, the box slipped from my hand, and I fell trying to catch it. When I looked up, Michael was watching from the window, and I swear I heard him say, 'Are you ok?' I was so shocked and scared all I could do was shake my head and stutter 'I . . . I'm fine.' And then he disappeared. It was really creepy. I'm not scared and still do my deliveries, but I haven't seen him since. I don't even know how I could have heard him. It's a long way between the square and the window. I don't think the window was even open."

"Wait, you've *seen* him?" asked Tia. "I don't believe it. What was he like? Were you scared? Could you see through him? How many times did you see him? Did you ever talk to him?"

"Woah, slow down, Tia. Take a breath, honey," interrupted Dwayne.

Tia dropped into a camp chair. She looked confused.

Bel replied, "Yes, I have seen him. I wasn't scared but a little freaked. No, I couldn't see through him. I've seen him five or six times. He only spoke to me once."

"I think it would be really cool to see a ghost," stated Dwayne.

"Me too," piped in Jason and Anna, almost in unison.

"I think we should sit around the town square tonight, after the concert, and see if he shows up," suggested Dwayne. "Or would that freak you out too much, Tia?"

"Bel, if there is a ghost — and I'm not saying you're a liar, I'm just a sceptic — do you think he would be upset if we were hanging out in the town square trying to see him in the window?" I asked.

"I don't think so," replied Bel. "But," she paused. "If you do decide to try and see him, promise me you won't get too close to the funeral home."

"What's so big about the funeral home?" Jason asked. "I've been in a couple of them before. It's no big deal."

"Just promise me you'll keep a safe distance. Mr. O'Reagan has made it very clear a few times that he doesn't take to kindly to people intruding on his property. One year, some concert people parked in his parking lot, and they found their tires slashed and a note on their car that simply said

"No Parking." And there's been a few other things. Just promise to stay away. Please." She was almost pleading.

Jason put up his hands. "Ok, no funeral home. Just the town square."

Dwayne looked down at his watch. "It's already four thirty," he said. "If we want to have any chance of a decent seat for Ed Sheeran, we should get on the next bus."

"Have fun at the concert," Bel said as she got up, and then she was off, skipping towards the barn. I marvelled at how she always seemed so upbeat and full of energy, even though she got up at four each morning.

CHAPTER 15

THE BUS WASN'T very full. I guessed most had already made their way to the festival for the earlier concerts. We could have each had a seat to ourselves, but I was the only one to sit alone. I had ten minutes of quiet, and a lot to think about. Jason and I had talked, but I still had unresolved feelings. It felt good that Anna knew everything now. But I still felt a shot of jealousy seeing them together. Was I still in love with Jason? I didn't think so, but then why was I still a little jealous? Maybe it was just that they seemed so happy together. Like Jason and I had been.

We were dropped off right in front of the gate. There was a huge crowd. I knew they had sold all fifty thousand tickets to this year's festival.

We weaved our way through the crowd following the wake left in Dwayne's path. It was nice having a big guy to lead the way. The closer we got to the middle of the crowd, the tighter people were packed. But Dwayne, being over six feet tall, led us to a good spot. Enough room for all of us to sit without being packed in like sardines, and just a little further back and to the right from where we had sat the night before. Still close enough for a good view of the stage, and close enough to the sound crew to know we would get great sound.

With half an hour until the first act, Dwayne and Tia offered to get supper for us.

After they left, there was an awkward silence. I opened my mouth to say something but closed it, not knowing what to say. After a couple of minutes I said, "Okay, so now that everything is out in the open, where do we go from here?"

"I have no idea," responded Anna. "I'm happy I finally know what happened, but now I'm wondering if you're still in love with Jason, or mad at him, or if you're mad at me for dating him. I don't even know if we're still friends."

"I'm not mad at anyone," I paused. "Not anymore anyway." I chose my words carefully so that my emotions wouldn't cause me to say something I couldn't take back.

"Jason, you will always have a place in my heart, and hopefully my life, but we can't go back, that's for sure. Too much has happened between us. To say I don't still love you would, I don't know, almost be a lie, because I do — but more as someone from my past. I still care about you, but we can never be together again. I know that now.

"Anna, I love you. I always will, and I'm not mad at you for dating Jason. I was scared for you when you first started dating, but you two are so good together. I could never do anything to change that, and I wouldn't want too. And I don't think Jason would ever do anything to hurt you. I also think that he's grown enough that his parents wouldn't be able to interfere, either. Honestly, I'm happy for you guys. I see the way you are together, and I hope I never come between you. Anna, I pray you guys can move past what happened between Jason and me. I know he didn't tell you because he thought I did, and that you already knew. I didn't tell you because I didn't want to hurt Jason. I hope you understand."

I was crying again. I hoped no one else was listening and watching. Anna and Jason were both in tears, but Jason was doing a better job at holding them back than Anna and I. Anna reached out and gave me a big hug. "Oh, Beth. I'll always be your friend. Jason and I talked, a lot, and we're okay. We can both move through this. Our concern is for you."

"Yeah, Beth," Jason interjected, "I'm so sorry I hurt you like that. I hope you can forgive me. I hope we can still be friends."

We all hugged, and cried. "I'm so glad we finally worked all this out." I sobbed.

We were still in an embrace when we heard someone clear their throat. We looked up and Tia and Dwayne were standing there with their hands full of food.

"Well, can we get a little help here, or are you still needing more time alone? We got everything on the list, and the food is getting cold." Tia said it all with a great big smile on her face. "I'm so happy to see you all hugging like that!"

"All is good," I told her. "Friends forever."

Just then Passenger and the Darkness struck the first chord of their set. We all stayed seated and ate our dinner. The mood had shifted, lightened. It felt almost like it used to — almost.

As I ate, I caught Tia's eye and whispered, "Thank you." She smiled, nodded, and then turned to Dwayne and said something I couldn't hear. Dwayne looked at me and smiled. It was good to have friends who cared about me, and about each other.

The music was pretty good. I let the emotions of the day fall away and the music wash over me. I danced. I laughed. We all did. There were smiles and laughter and a few hugs. We were going to be alright. It was like we were getting a fresh start.

The band played for about forty-five minutes, and Ed Sheeran joined them for their last song. Ed sang every song I knew and a few I didn't. About an hour in, the first notes to "The Joker and The Queen" were struck, and the crowd went wild. Fifty thousand people cheered and screamed as Taylor Swift walked onto the stage. She not only performed their hit song but stayed and sang a couple more with Ed, including my favourite, "Everything Has Changed." It was a fantastic concert! After Taylor had sung a few songs, she asked the audience, "Are y'all gonna stay for my concert on Sunday?" The crowd erupted with a resounding "YES!" Then Ed continued his show.

The music made me forget the events of the day. I didn't have a care in the world. I felt the stress leave my body, once and for all. All the anxiety, and anger, and sadness lifted from my spirit. I let out a happy scream. I looked around, and my friends were all smiling at me.

The concert finished with a fifteen-minute fireworks display. There were big boomers, and sparkly trailers, reds and greens and blues and even some multicoloured ones. The display ended with a waterfall of colour dropping from a point high above the stage.

CHAPTER 16

WE FOLLOWED THE crowd out through the lower gate. It took about fifteen minutes before we were on the street and able to gather to talk. The plan was to hang out in the town square to watch for the ghost. I was pretty sceptical, but I figured, why not? As long as we didn't go into the funeral home, as we'd promised Bel.

"So, do we walk, or see if the bus will drop us off on the way by?" I asked the group.

"We could walk, it isn't that far, maybe three miles or so," Dwayne said.

"If we took the bus, we would be there faster," replied Tia. "Besides, we'll have to walk the four or five miles back to the farm afterwards. I'm not up for that much walking." I knew Tia wasn't really up for this whole adventure, so I supported her in taking the bus. Besides, I was feeling tired from all the emotions of the day.

As we boarded the bus, Jason asked the driver if he would drop us off at the town square. We took seats near the front, and five minutes later, got off right next to the fountain. I could see the funeral home, and it was even creepier in the dark, especially with the glow of some soft lighting coming from behind the windows. I guessed that there were a few security lights on inside.

Bel had told us that she was close to the fountain when she'd had an encounter with the ghost, so we decided to hang out there. It was as good a place as any, I figured. Besides, that's where the benches were, and they gave a great view of the windows.

"I hope we see the ghost," Dwayne said, as he sat on one of the benches.

"Not me," shot Tia. "I think this is all too creepy."

"Don't worry, Tia," I told her. "You just hang on to that strong man of yours. He'll protect you if the ghost shows up and tries anything." We all laughed. I thought to myself, *This finally feels right. All of us together as friends, the drama behind us.*

"What's your plan if the ghost shows up?" asked Anna. I knew she thought this whole thing was a waste of time. Like me, she didn't believe in actual ghosts. We were both just here to see how far the guys were willing to take it. My only fear was that we were close to O'Reagan's, and I found it creepy. I made sure that I sat where I could keep an eye on it.

"I don't know what I'll do." Jason talked through a plan out loud. "If I see him, I think I'll wave and see if he waves back. Bel said he was friendly when she saw him, so I don't think we need to be afraid of him."

"I hope you and Bel are right," pouted Tia. "If he shows up, I'll run away."

We all laughed. "I've got your back, sweetie," Dwayne promised, and he put his strong arm around her shoulders, pulling her in tight. He leaned down and gave her a kiss on the top of her head.

After about fifteen minutes, Anna got up and walked around a bit. She didn't go far, just weaved through the trees, walking around the fountain and back. We stopped paying attention, and then she was gone. I was the first to notice that she hadn't come back, that it had been several minutes since I'd seen her.

"Where's Anna?" I asked. And then everyone looked at each other. She'd been gone for several minutes.

"Anna," Jason called. "Where are you? Come on, honey, don't do this to us, it's not funny." We all waited a beat, but there was no response. "We need to find her," Jason said as he stood up.

"I'm sure she's just hiding on us, waiting to jump out and scare us," Tia assured him.

We called for her and looked around, then all met back near the fountain. Jason was really concerned by now. "Anna!" he yelled, as we stood together by the fountain. "This isn't funny. Please come out."

That's when I saw her, sneaking through the maze of trees and trash cans, making a beeline for Jason. I stepped back just as Anna leaped from the shadows and shoved Jason from the side, and he tripped over the edge of the fountain and landed with a huge splash! Everyone got sprayed with the cool water. Anna stood there laughing. Jason was sputtering and thrashing as he stood up, knee deep in the fountain with the little nude dude peeing on his head. I wish I'd thought to take a picture.

"What the hell?" Jason scolded. "That wasn't funny." After he collected himself, his voice softened, and he waded towards her. "At least help me out," he said to Anna. As he stepped out of the fountain, holding Anna's hand, his expression changed to a grin. Next thing I knew, he stooped down, picked her up, and threw her in. Anna flopped in the water and came up with her hair dripping. "Oh, you're gonna get it now," she laughed and splashed him. Then we all piled into the fountain, thoughts of the ghost disappearing from our thoughts.

We were still splashing and chasing each other through the water, round and round the statue, when — seemingly out of nowhere — we heard, "Hey, what do you think you're doing? Get out of the fountain!"

I spun to see the sheriff standing a few feet away. We all stopped and sheepishly climbed out of the fountain.

"We're sorry, officer. We didn't mean any harm. We were just blowing off a little steam," I offered.

"Can't you guys read?" Sheriff Johnson asked us, pointing to a sign I hadn't noticed. It read: Absolutely No Persons or Pets in the Fountain.

"Oh," Anna responded. "I'm sorry, sir. It was my fault. I snuck up from behind and pushed him in." She pointed to Jason. "It was just a joke, and then one thing led to another. I never even noticed the sign until just now. Please, forgive us."

"It's Beth, isn't it?" He asked me. "We, uh, ran into each other before, didn't we? Can I please see some ID for each of you?" We all reached into our pockets and handed him our driver's licenses. He took a minute or two to look at them, compared our pictures to our faces, and then handed them back. "Am I correct in assuming you are here for the festival?" he asked.

"Yes, officer," responded Jason.

"And where are you staying?" Johnson asked.

"We have a site out at the farm," Jason told him.

"Then I suggest you head over there and get some sleep. Is your car parked close by?" He asked us.

"No, sir." Jason continued to be our spokesperson. "We were going to walk back."

"I don't think that's a good idea," he replied. "There are black bears and other animals around. I think I'd better drive you. Come on, my car's just over there. It'll be a tight fit, but I think we can manage for such a short trip."

He led us to a Ford Bronco with a light bar on top. When I saw it, I thought of all the B-movies I'd seen where the small-town sheriff drove a brown Ford Bronco just like this.

We piled in, and he drove us to the farm. Me in the front, and the rest in the back seat. When we arrived, we realized that the back doors didn't open from the inside. The sheriff got out and opened the door on his side, and I followed suit on mine. Once we were all out, the sheriff said, "Have a nice night, folks. Welcome to Harrington. I trust I won't see you playing in the fountain again."

"No sir," I said. "Thank you for the ride. We really appreciate it."

With that, Sheriff Johnson got back in the Bronco and drove off. We all sighed in relief.

"Man, I thought we were going to be in trouble!" laughed Tia.

"Me too," said Anna. And then we all broke out into laughter.

We realized it was almost one a.m., so we were careful to be quiet as we picked our way through the campground to the purple glow of Jason's tent. I thought again how smart he had been to bring the coloured glow sticks.

We whispered good nights to each other. Anna gave me a big hug and quietly said, "I'm so glad we got to talk today." Then we all climbed into our tents and fell asleep.

CHAPTER 17

I WOKE UP ON Friday at six a.m. and was already sweating. A hot, humid air mass had swept in overnight, and it was already in the mid-eighties according to a thermometer on the tent one campsite over. It felt more like a hundred. I was still tired from being out so late the night before, but it was way too hot to sleep. I crawled out of the tent and went immediately to the cooler, hoping there would still be some ice left and that the water would be cold. Thank God it was.

As I sat in my camp chair and drank in the cool liquid, Tia and Dwayne also awoke and joined me.

"We should go for a swim this morning," I suggested, remembering how cool the lake was from my fishing trip a couple of days before. "There's a small beach we can walk to easily."

"That sounds like a great idea!" exclaimed Dwayne. "It's so hot this morning, I bet we could fry bacon and eggs on the rocks without even building a fire."

About twenty minutes later, Anna and Jason emerged from their tent. We all put on our swimsuits and walked down to the beach.

"Hey, Anna, are you going to push Dwayne in the water again?" I joked.

"Not this morning, but you never know what'll happen if we go by the fountain again," she laughed.

We splashed and swam in the water for a bit and then spread out our towels on the small beach and relaxed in the early morning sun. The heat didn't seem quite as bad here next to the lake.

"The sheriff wasn't so keen on finding us in the fountain last night," started Dwayne. "I'm glad he didn't make a thing about it."

"You and me both," said Jason. "I've seen enough of law enforcement this trip already. First the border guards, then the cop who got me for speeding, and now the sheriff last night. I'll be lucky if they ever let me in the States again."

"At least the cop who pulled you over for speeding was nice. Officer Alice something wasn't it?" I asked.

"Yeah, Alice Maxwell. I still have her card in my wallet," Jason told us.

"I'm just happy we didn't see a ghost last night," Tia offered. "I'm not sure if I'd have stopped running yet!" We all laughed.

"I was hoping we would see it," claimed Jason, "but I guess it wasn't meant to be. It's likely just a local myth, anyway. Bel was probably just pulling our chains."

"I'm not so sure, Jason," Dwayne interjected. "I was talking to a few people at the festival last night, and most of them had heard the story about the funeral-home owner, Conor O'Reagan, and the little boy. They all seemed to concur that there is a ghost. One even claimed to have seen it in the window."

"I think it's all just a story," I said. "I mean, the festival happens every year. A local starts a rumour and it spreads like wildfire through the visitors. Pretty soon it becomes a legend. I'm sure there is some truth to the death of the little boy, but a ghost? Really? I find that hard to believe."

"I don't know," Dwayne defended. "First Bel, then a number of people at the festival all share the same story, and Bel lives here. She should know. Besides, she says that she's even heard it talk to her. I believe her. You also said you thought you saw a little boy in the window when the funeral home was empty. And that was before we even knew the story!"

"Well, I guess we'll never know," I said. "We tried and failed last night, and I don't think sitting around the town square again is a great idea after the sheriff ran us off last night."

That seemed to end the talk about the ghost. We all took another quick dip in the lake and then headed back to the farm to make breakfast. We opted for a light breakfast of yogourt from the cooler and cereal with milk.

After breakfast, we each made our way up to the showers. I was glad for the cool water this morning. I was the last one back to the campsite, and when I arrived, everyone was still talking about the ghost.

"I think we could easily get inside," I heard Dwayne say as I approached.

"And just how are we supposed to do that?" Tia retorted. "It'll be closed and all locked up, and it's not like you're going to knock on the door and ask the owner for permission to spend the night in his funeral home, so you can try and see a ghost."

"I have one of these." Dwayne pulled a small gun-like object from his pocket.

"What is that?" I jumped in.

"This is a lock pick gun. It will open any tumbler lock on the market." Dwayne handed me the tool.

I took it and looked it over. It seemed to be made of steel. There was a handle and trigger, like a gun with no barrel. Instead, there was an attachment you could slide into a door lock and when you pushed the trigger the little needle part moved back and forth.

"Where on earth did you get this — and why did you get it?"

"It's amazing what you can buy on Amazon," Dwayne grinned. "I saw it on a Facebook ad and figured it might come in handy if I ever locked myself out. It works pretty well. I can open the door to my house in under sixty seconds."

"Well, I don't think we should do it. Breaking and entering is a much bigger deal than splashing around in the fountain. If we got caught, we would all go to jail," I warned. "I'm with Tia. I can't believe we are actually even having this discussion."

"I'm in," Jason said. "We won't do anything inside but look around, and I bet they don't even have an up-to-date security system. In this small town, I doubt there's much crime. Besides, who would want to break into a funeral home? There'd be nothing to steal but office supplies and dead bodies. What do you think, Anna? Will you come with us?"

"Uh, I don't know," Anna started. "I don't think it's a great idea. I mean, we saw the owner at a house across the street. I think that's where he lives. He could see the front doors from his living room."

"We would park up the street and go in through the back." Jason had obviously been thinking about it, as he had a plan all figured out.

"So, it's a 2–2 vote, with one undecided," I said. "That means we don't do it. Now, let's move on to the important stuff. I noticed a couple of pop-up shops near the festival. I think Tia and I need to check them out before the concert today. I was thinking we could go to Annie's for lunch and then do a little shopping before the gates open. What do you think, Tia?"

"Ooo, that sounds like fun!" Tia said gleefully.

I knew I could count on Tia to go shopping. I just hoped that this change in topic would put an end to the break-and-enter talk. I didn't want the guys to think I was scared of the funeral home, but I was.

I was looking forward to today's lineup. Maren Morris was up first at two o'clock, followed by Loote and then Justin Bieber. Ava Max would start the evening session at seven and then Ariana Grande was the headliner.

We left the farm around eleven and headed to the pop-up shops. They were simple construction trailers parked near the gates. Our plan was to park and then walk to town for lunch.

The first shop was filled with branded festival souvenirs. They had every kind of apparel you could imagine. Tia and I each got a festival T-shirt with a list of all the bands on the back. Dwayne bought a ball cap. Jason and Anna didn't buy anything. I also found a couple of shot glasses for my collection.

The second shop focused more on knick-knacks. I wandered around and saw a few things that were amusing, including a "Bieber Bong." I showed it to Anna, who also thought it was funny. As we were looking around, a big clap of thunder rang through the air. Followed by another and another. And then we heard the sound of hail pounding on the roof of the trailer. I looked out the window and was amazed at how hard it was hailing. Thankfully, the largest hail stones were only the size of a pea, but there were a lot of them. Then it turned to rain.

"I guess we get to shop a little longer," giggled Tia, picking up a golf umbrella with "Mainestock" on every other panel. About ten minutes later, the rain stopped as quickly as it had started, and we exited the trailer to find that the temperature had dropped by about ten degrees, and the humidity had broken. It was a beautiful afternoon.

We put our purchases in the Pilot, with the exception of the umbrella. "Just in case," Tia said. Then it was off to town for lunch at Annie's. Sally served us once again and was as cheerful as she had been the first time we ate there.

After lunch we made our way back to the festival grounds. We only had to wait about fifteen minutes to get in the gate, and we were able to get a spot in the same area we'd been in before: centre stage near the sound engineers. My mind was wandering as I watched the few clouds in the sky. I was amazed at how quickly the grass had dried out after the sudden downpour. I snapped out of my own thoughts when I heard Jason say, "Earth to Beth."

"Oh sorry," I said. "I was lost in my thoughts. What's up?"

"Dwayne, Anna, and I were talking on the walk back, and I think we want to see if we can get into the funeral home," he informed me.

I looked at Tia. She shrugged and shook her head.

"What is your fascination with seeing a ghost?" I asked. "We can't just go breaking into buildings. What if we get caught? Do you think the sheriff will let us off with just another warning? I don't. I think we end up in jail. I think it's a terrible idea and I don't want to do it."

"We talked about that too," Jason continued. "If anyone doesn't want to do it, they can take the bus back to the farm, and we'll join them there just before dawn."

"Well, then, I guess I'm taking the bus back to the farm," I sighed. "I'm not risking jail time to see some ghost. I don't believe in ghosts, but I do believe in Sheriff Alex Johnson. And I believe he won't hesitate to throw us in his jail. What about you, Tia? Are you on board with their lame-brained plan?"

"I don't know, maybe?" she said.

I just shook my head. "I think I need a candied apple. I'll be back in a few minutes," I said, and I walked off, disgusted and worried.

CHAPTER 18

I BOUGHT MY CANDIED apple and a bottle of water and made my way back to my friends. Maren Morris took the stage just before I got back, and I let go of my thoughts about the funeral home and enjoyed the music. No one said anything further about their plan. We all just enjoyed the music.

Loote was next, a duo. Both artists sounded good, and I enjoyed them although I didn't know their music. There was a short break scheduled before Justin Bieber. Anna took the opportunity to talk to me.

"Come on Beth, won't you change your mind? I don't want you going back to the farm by yourself. Tia decided she was in. It's not like we're going to break anything or steal something. We're just going to pick the lock and see what we can see. Dwayne says he can pick the lock with his gadget really quickly, and if an alarm goes off, we run. I don't believe in ghosts, but I think it would be neat to see the funeral home at night!"

"Really Anna? Now you're on board enough to try and convince me?" I asked her. "What happens if we do get caught? Besides, I have a bad feeling about the funeral home. Something about the owner gives me the creeps."

"If we stay together, what can go wrong?" Anna asked. "We'll be careful. The plan is to see if there's a back door to the church. The guys figure that'll be the oldest lock and easiest to pick. Then we can just look around. We'll use our phones as flashlights, find a good spot to sit and wait and see what happens. They said we'd leave before dawn, while it's still dark. Please come with us."

"I'll think about it, but I'm telling you, this is a bad idea," I cautioned.

Anna left me alone to think, and Justin Bieber took the stage. I remembered hearing how he had been discovered after he posted a video online. Usher somehow heard him, and the rest, as they say, was history. I also remembered that Justin had turned into a spoiled brat, but then somewhere along the line, he found religion. I'd heard he even sang at some churches on a worship team. Justin had married Stephen Baldwin's daughter Hailey last year. I knew a few of his songs, like "Baby" and "Love Yourself."

I tried to put the thought of the funeral home out of my mind, without success. I almost didn't notice Ed Sheeran walk out on stage in a surprise appearance. He and Bieber sang a song together that I didn't know was a Bieber tune, "I Don't Care." Finally, the plan left my thoughts as I listened to the duet.

There was a short break to reset the stage for the main event, Ariana Grande. I loved her music. I'd first really heard her when she played at the Music Video Awards last year. Anna had invited me over to watch, and even though things were weird between us, I went. I was glad I did, because I loved Ariana's performance. We hadn't danced then, but I was hoping to dance tonight.

At seven sharp, Ava Max took the stage. She was pretty good but not good enough to stop my brain from going back to the funeral home. Despite my fears, I didn't want to be a downer, and I didn't want to go back to the farm alone. I got Anna's attention and said, "OK, I'm in. But I run at the first sign of trouble."

"That's awesome!" Anna said. She called to Jason above the noise "Beth is in!"

"Great!" Jason said. "That's everyone then."

I had trouble enjoying the Ariana Grande concert. It ended at about ten thirty, and we made our way to the car.

"OK, so here's the plan," Dwayne began. "We're going to drive through town and park on the other side of O'Reagan's. Then we go to the back and check the doors. If we get lucky, they forgot to lock one and it's easy-peasy. If not, we try to pick the lock in the back of the chapel, if there is one. We don't go up the side or out front and risk being seen."

"We need to be really quiet too," interjected Dwayne. "No talking or giggling."

Jason continued, "Once we're inside, we wait for a minute or two, in case there's an alarm. If one goes off, we bolt and don't look back. If not, we can go in and take a look around. We'll find a good spot to sit and watch, maybe close to the morgue. We wait a while, if we don't see anything, we leave. Sound ok?"

"I'm still not okay with this," I protested. "What if there are cameras or something?"

"We'll look for them. If we see any, we leave. It's simple," Dwayne answered. I sighed a heavy sigh and rolled my eyes.

"Any other questions?" asked Jason. No one spoke. "Alright, then. Let's head over."

He started the engine and followed the last bit of traffic out of the parking lot. He drove slower than usual and made his way to the far end of town, parking about a hundred yards from the funeral home. We all just sat there in silence. Waiting for someone to say something or make a move.

It was almost midnight when Jason finally stirred. We hadn't seen a car or a person in almost thirty minutes. He turned and said, "All set?"

"I'm still saying that this is a bad idea. Why don't we just go to the farm and get some sleep. We can come tomorrow in the daylight. Maybe Mr. O'Reagan would give us a tour or something?"

"It needs to be at night," replied Jason. "Ghosts don't show themselves during the day with a lot of people around." Like he knew what he was talking about. Who did he think he was? A Ghostbuster?

We slowly got out of the car and shut the doors as quietly as we could, and gathered on the sidewalk. "OK, single file. No talking. Ready?" Jason asked. We all nodded. "Let's go." And we were off. We cut diagonally across the back of the funeral home towards the church, moving slowly and silently.

We were in luck. The door at the back of the church looked old, and so did the lock. Jason moved aside, and Dwayne knelt down in front of the door. He took out the gun thing, screwed on a long needle-like piece below a metal stick that stuck out at the top, and inserted it into the lock. He pulled the trigger a couple of times and tried the door. Nothing. He tried again and still nothing. He replaced the needle and tried again. This time the knob turned. He looked back at us, and Jason gave him a thumbs up. He pushed the door open a crack and waited. There was no siren, no flashing lights, nothing. He stood up, pushed the door open a little further and then stood back. Jason stepped forward and went inside. No one else moved for a good twenty seconds. Then Anna went in, then Dwayne, followed by Tia. I was alone outside. I looked around one last time and then stepped inside the church, carefully closing the door behind me.

CHAPTER 19

It was almost black inside the chapel's back door, the only light the dim red glow of the exit sign. None of us moved or spoke for a good five minutes. We stood so close to each other, it got really warm. I kept expecting to hear an alarm or the siren of the sheriff's car, but nothing happened. All of a sudden, Jason turned on his phone's flashlight app and pointed it at the floor in front of us. He slowly moved it upwards and around in a circle, taking in the small rear entry.

There was a set of stairs to our left leading down into the basement and a door directly in front of us. There were no windows, which is why it was so dark. Jason shone the light along the ceiling.

"Just checking for cameras or motion sensors. Okay," he whispered, "I'm going to slowly open the door. You guys stay right here and be ready to run if an alarm goes off."

He slowly moved to the door and gripped the doorknob, turning it and then pulling it in towards us. I don't think I even took a breath until he had it open all the way. We all waited for a minute, but nothing happened. Without a word, Jason stepped through the door. It was still very dark in the entry, but we could see Jason's silhouette through the door. We watched as he slowly shone his light around the chapel. I could make out a few pews from where I stood, but nothing else.

"No sign of an alarm. Come on in," Jason quietly called.

We slowly walked forward. I still couldn't believe we were actually doing this.

"If you turn on your lights, keep them pointed at the floor," Jason directed, "there's less chance someone will see them."

We all turned on our flashlights and fanned out, walking around what appeared to be the main sanctuary. There were two rows of pews with a centre aisle. Perfect for a wedding or a funeral procession. Each row was about forty pews long and twenty feet wide. There was a balcony at the back that looked to hold another two rows of eight or ten pews. Stained glass windows lined each wall, which I found funny because I hadn't seen them from outside. I went through a door to the left of the stage and saw a hallway that ran the width of the sanctuary. To my left was a hallway to the front of the church, and straight ahead was another door. I wasn't going through it by myself.

I went back into the main sanctuary. Dwayne and Tia had opened the door on the other side. "There's a hall that runs up to the front," Dwayne said, "and then a shorter one that leads behind the stage to a big bathtub or something."

"It's called a baptismal," I informed them. "It's used to baptize Christians." I remembered when I was baptised as a teenager. It seemed like a lifetime ago. I hadn't been to church since . . . well, since graduation. After Jason took off, and my pregnancy scare, I pretty much gave up on church, only going with my parents at Christmas, Easter, and Thanksgiving. I was still a Christian, but my connection to the church had almost vanished. I was ashamed of what had happened and didn't want to face the gossip and wondering eyes if someone knew. Church can be great, but sometimes it can be awful, too.

On the stage there were several chairs, a cross, and a podium, along with several microphone stands and music stands. At the front of the stage, on the main floor, was a table — a communion table, I recalled.

Jason and Anna walked towards us from the back of the church. "Nothing up here but the door and stairs to the balcony," Anna reported. "There's a hole in the ceiling, too. I think it must be where the bell used to be."

"I found another door, but I didn't open it. It might lead to the funeral home," I guessed.

We slowly moved towards the door as a group. Once again, Jason led the way. When we got to the door, Jason had us all turn off our phones, just in case. Dwayne cautiously opened the door with his lock pick, and we waited. Nothing again, so we turned our lights back on. I noticed that Tia was practically in Dwayne's back pocket. She looked as white as the ghost we were trying to find.

A cold breeze swept past that made me shiver. I could have sworn I heard the words "get out now" being carried on the breeze. The hair stood up on my arms and the back of my neck. "Does anyone else feel a cold draft?" I asked. No one responded.

As we looked down the hall we saw several doors off to the right, across from a row of opaque windows on the left, overlooking the parking lot. "OK, everyone, turn off your lights," Jason ordered us. "We don't want someone calling the police because they see a bunch of flashlights moving around." We all complied. A little light filtered into the windows from the streetlights across the parking lot, and there were two small, dim lights at each end of the hall.

When our eyes finally adjusted to the dim light, and we could see enough to get around, we approached the first door together. Dwayne opened it, stepped into the room, turned on his light and looked around. I followed him in. The room was fairly small, about ten feet by twelve. The perimeter was lined with shelves filled with boxes and other supplies. A storage room. No windows, only a vent high on the wall.

When I turned to leave, I realized Jason and Anna weren't with us. They must have continued down the hall. I went back out to the hall and saw that the next door was open. I found Jason and Anna in what appeared to be a board room. There was a large table and eight chairs, and a Keurig machine sitting on a counter that ran along one end. There was a water cooler and a large screen TV on the wall opposite the counter. There was one window and a door marked with another exit sign. Nothing much to see.

Then, a set of steel double doors. The sign on the right hand one read "Morgue." It was locked. Dwayne pulled out his lock pick gun and opened it in under thirty seconds. He looked at Jason, who nodded, and then we all entered.

The first thing that struck me was the heavy, sweet smell. It wasn't disgusting, but not pleasant either. Then it hit me. "It smells kinda like that stuff the janitors back at FHS used to put on the floor when they polished them — like a cherry smell."

"That's it," squealed Tia. "I couldn't place it until you said that, but you're right. It smells like FHS after the students left and the cleaning staff were making their rounds."

"I was thinking more like the Rainbow Carwash up on Prospect Street," interjected Dwayne.

"You're all right," said Jason.

The second thing I noticed was how sterile the room was, and how large. All the counters were stainless steel. The floor was tile and had five drains, four forming the corners of a large square, and one in the centre. Along the wall to the right was a row of stainless steel sinks with large vats between them, a tube extending out of each. Between the door and the wall of sinks was a line of cabinets that looked like Dad's tool chest. I opened a drawer and saw that it was filled with scissors. Another was filled with knives — scalpels, I thought, though I'd never seen one before except in the movies.

As I shone my light ahead of me, I saw half a dozen stainless steel gurneys. They had troughs running across the tops and sides, and holes connected to tubes in the bottoms. Straight ahead was a bank of doors on the wall, mini walk-in fridge doors just like in the ghost town mortuary. Here, there were twelve of them. To the left of the small doors was another door with an exit sign.

We had all spread out, and everyone was looking at something different. "This is really creepy," breathed Tia as she hung tightly to Dwayne.

Along the last wall was a door marked Crematorium. On either side were shelves lined with many boxes and urns of all shapes and sizes.

Jason was at the exit door on the back wall with Anna. He opened it and looked in. "It's the garage." He told us.

"Nothing in there but a few tools and the hearse." He closed the door once again and then turned to the wall of fridge doors.

"I don't think we should," Anna piped in. "What if there are bodies in there? Or a ghost?"

Jason stopped and looked at her and then turned towards the crematorium. The whole thing was ominous. The only light was our phones and the exit sign. We were in the morgue. I shuddered at the thought of how many dead people came through here. I wondered if there were bodies in the wall right now. I followed Jason and Anna to the crematorium door.

Dwayne moved to follow us when Tia grabbed his arm, "Don't. Let's just stay here, back a little. Just in case."

Anna reached for the door this time. It swung inward with ease. As it did, I felt another cool draft sweep over me. *"Run,"* I thought I heard.

"Did you hear that?" I asked.

"Hear what," Anna responded.

"When the draft blew by, I heard a voice whisper 'run.'"

"Are you sure?" It was Tia, now hiding behind Dwayne.

"Not really. But I think so. It's the second time I've felt a draft and thought I heard a voice. Maybe it's just my imagination," I said. "Ok guys, I'm really getting creeped out. Can we go now? We got in, looked around and saw nothing. No harm, no foul. If we go now, no one will know we were even here."

"Give me a minute," Jason said as he walked into the crematorium. A light went on. It must have been on a motion sensor. "Guys, come see this!" he called.

We all followed Jason into the crematorium. Inside was a large concrete and steel box. It was about seven feet tall, six feet wide and fifteen feet long. There was a door in one end about three feet square starting about three feet off the floor. A number of pipes came out of it on the top with several gauges attached. Attached to one side was a computer screen and a few more gauges. Jason tapped a keyboard and the screen lit up.

"I don't think that's a good idea," Dwayne advised. "We don't want to break anything, or God forbid, start it up."

Along with what I thought was the actual cremation chamber, I saw several long brooms and poles, what appeared to be a hydraulic lift, some cupboards, and a long counter with a fume hood at the far end. I walked over to the fume hood and read a sign stuck to a big cylinder: Bone Pulveriser, it read.

"Why do you suppose they need that?" I asked.

Jason explained: "Some bones don't actually burn up, so they have to grind them up and mix them into the ashes."

I was horrified. It was bad enough to think that someone wanted to be burned, but then to have to grind them up too!

"Okay, I'm getting out of here." Tia went to the door, looked back to see if we would follow, and stepped out. I followed, then Dwayne and Anna. Jason was the last to leave, closing the door behind him.

"I just want to look in the actual funeral home and then we can go." Jason told us. "Are we good to look around for a few more minutes?"

"I don't know Jason," Dwayne protested. "Haven't we seen enough? Tia is scared and I'll admit that I'm a little creeped out too. Maybe we should go, like Beth said."

"Just a few more minutes guys. Please?" Jason pleaded. "We've come this far, what will a few more minutes hurt?

Maybe the ghost of the boy lives in the funeral home itself. Let's take a vote. I'm going. Who's with me?"

Anna slowly put up her hand. Dwayne looked at Tia who nodded.

"Ten more minutes," I said.

CHAPTER 20

THE DOOR BACK into the funeral home opened easily. We paused again, waiting for any sign of an alarm. Nothing. Jason stepped across the threshold and Anna followed. I sighed and followed them through. Tia and Dwayne came behind me.

I saw movement in my peripheral vision to my right. I gasped and turned to look. Nothing.

"What's wrong?" Tia sounded concerned. We were all on edge.

"I . . . I could have sworn I saw someone." I replied. "My imagination must really be working overtime."

"You saw the ghost?" Jason exclaimed. "Where?"

"I'm not sure," I stammered, still spooked. "I was sure I saw someone — or something — move over there." We all turned our phones in the direction I pointed, but there was no sign of a ghost, or of anything. "OK, we've seen the funeral home part. Let's go now."

"Come on, Beth," Dwayne responded. "Don't back out now. There's no one here and obviously no alarm. Let's at least look around a little. Give it a few more minutes so we can scope it out. Who knows, maybe you did see a ghost, and it's just hiding." He finished with a sinister little laugh that I didn't find funny.

"OK, let's get this over with," I said reluctantly.

To our right was an alcove with two doors. Bathrooms.

"Frig!" Tia groaned. "My phone is dead. I don't have a light."

"Sorry, honey, just stick close to me. I'll protect you. You can even hold mine if it makes you feel better," Dwayne offered his phone to Tia, who took it gratefully.

To our immediate left a coat rack ran up the wall, with an exit door beyond it. There were two security lights above the coat rack giving us a little bit of light. I turned off my phone to prolong the battery life.

Across the space, about twenty feet in front of us, was a door with a sign above it. I walked across so I could see. It read Family Room. I stopped at the door and Anna bumped into me. I screamed and jumped, turning around, ready to fight. I hadn't realized that she and Jason had followed me over.

"Woah, it's just me," Anna defended. "Sorry I scared you, but I know who I want to walk around with, now. You look ready to kick some serious butt!"

Jason and Anna both laughed hard. I started to laugh too. The tension finally fell away.

After I collected myself, I opened the door. We walked into a room furnished much like a living room. There were a couple of couches and armchairs. A buffet and hutch stood at one end, with cups and saucers, mugs, and serving trays behind glass doors. It held a Keurig machine and a pod carousel. Beside that was a water cooler with plastic cups on top. A large window was adorned with curtains that looked to be out of the seventies. I went to the window and looked behind the curtains, just in case. Nothing.

Beside the family room was a smaller room marked Clergy, with a love seat, a pair of armchairs, a window, a small cupboard, and again, a Keurig machine and a water cooler.

At the front of the funeral home, near the main door, were two rooms. The reception room was to the left. A single chair sat behind the desk and along one wall was a large bank of filing cabinets. The other room was marked Funeral Director. Inside was a large solid wood desk, a chair, a filing cabinet, a computer and a printer.

Directly in front of the main door and back about thirty feet was a grand staircase. Inside the door was a rack of donation cards from various charitable organizations.

As I came out of the Funeral Director's office, Dwayne was already climbing the stairs with Tia right behind him. Dwayne had his phone back and shone it on the stairs so they didn't trip going up.

"Do you guys know where Jason and Anna went?" I asked.

"Jason said they were going to check out the other end of the house. There was another double door by the family room." Dwayne told me. "They said they would meet up with us in a few minutes."

At the top of the stairs there was a small office on the right, along with another washroom. When we discovered nothing of interest, we looked at the other rooms. I assumed these used to be bedrooms when it was a house, but now they were all offices. Two of the four had ensuite bathrooms.

One of the larger offices had a sign on the door that read Conor O'Reagan: Owner. This room was slightly more tastefully decorated with a couple of plush armchairs, a large desk that Jason said was solid mahogany, a leather office chair, and a sofa against one wall. There was also a coffee nook complete with its own sink and bar fridge. On the desk was a large computer monitor, a mouse and keyboard, and stationery. This was obviously Conor's private workspace. I was surprised it wasn't locked.

We realized there was nothing much to look at up here other than desks, chairs, printers and some filing cabinets. Dwayne found a box of candy and took a peppermint, but other than that, nothing. As we returned to the top of the stairs, Dwayne stopped short. Tia ran right into him, again, and I almost ran into her. I was about to ask what was going on when I saw it.

There, standing on a landing halfway down the stairs, was a little boy. I couldn't make a sound beyond a gasp. My mouth hung open and I slowly pointed.

Tia was the first to react. A small squeak escaped her throat as she jumped further behind Dwayne, away from the boy. Dwayne got out a 'What the f —," before I managed a "Holy Crap!"

"Why didn't you leave when I told you to?" the boy asked. "I told you to go twice. Now it's too late. I don't think I can keep you all safe. He's really angry."

"Wh . . . who are you?" I stuttered.

"I'm Michael," he responded. "But you need to run. Now!"

Just then Jason appeared at the bottom of the stairs. "Holy Crap!" he said.

"I just said that," I told him.

"You guys need to leave, right now," warned Michael once again. "He's coming."

"What do you mean? Who's coming?" Jason asked.

"Conor," Michael answered. "You don't want to be here when he comes. He's so angry. He doesn't like it when people come here when they aren't supposed to. Please, leave."

"Okay, I think I've had enough." Dwayne asserted. "I'm out of here. I've seen the ghost, he told us to leave, I'm all good." Dwayne started down the stairs, Tia on his hip. I was too scared to move.

Dwayne skirted the little landing Michael stood on and joined Jason and Anna on the main floor.

"Beth, move!" It was Jason.

I snapped out of my trance and ran down the stairs. As I got to the landing I tripped and fell, tumbling right through Michael. I felt cold as I went through him. There was no question I'd just passed through a ghost.

"Wait," I said as Jason moved to pick me up. "Michael, was that you in the chapel and again in the hall that I heard? That I felt?"

"Yes. I was trying to get you to go before it was too late. And now, I think it is." Michael told me.

I got up and we all ran to the front door, the closest exit. We pushed on it, and it didn't open. Jason found the lock and turned it. Still nothing. The door would not budge.

"There's a door out the back, past the family room and through the kitchen." Anna instructed.

"What kitchen?" Tia asked.

"The one at the back, by the room with all the caskets. We found it while you were upstairs," Anna yelled as she led the way to the back.

We arrived at the back door and Anna slammed into the door and dropped to the ground. It didn't open. Dwayne pushed the bar and threw his shoulder into it. Nothing. It was like it was sealed shut. I was starting to panic now. How would we get out?

Then we heard a voice.

CHAPTER 21

"WELCOME TO MY home, my uninvited guests. I hope you enjoy your stay. It will be the last time you break into someone's house." Every hair on my body stood on end.

"Did you enjoy your tour of the premises? I see you made your way around most of it. You missed the basement of the chapel though." Again, a laugh. "But there will be time for you to see it before morning."

We were all frozen in place. I realized I was holding my breath and forced myself to suck in a lungful of air. The voice was deep and hollow and as sinister as a horror movie. It alone would have given me the creeps, but being locked in with it had us all terrified.

"The window!" I yelled. "Break the window!"

Jason grabbed a chair from around the small table in the kitchen and threw it at the window. It just bounced off. He tried again, this time swinging it himself instead of throwing it. It bounced off and hit Jason in the face. He fell to the floor with a thud, the chair landing on top of him.

"Jason!" screamed Anna.

Anna pulled the chair away from him, and he shook his head. His face was covered with blood. I grabbed a dish towel from the counter and wiped his face, assessing the damage. His nose was bleeding, and a cut above his eye dripped blood down the side of his face. I held the dish towel on his eyebrow.

"What do we do now?" I asked.

The voice returned. "Are you OK, big guy? I should have told you that the windows were shatterproof. I got tired of little boys throwing things through them. As for the doors, my lovely wife looked after those. She's a security expert, you know. Every door has been outfitted with electromagnetic locks that I control. No one can get in, no one can escape. You've put yourselves in quite a predicament don't you think? My dear, there is a small first aid kit under the sink. It should have what you need to get him patched up. I wouldn't want a little injury to get in the way of all the fun I have planned."

Michael appeared beside me. "You need to hide! Now! Try the church, he doesn't like it in there."

"Crap!" Anna said right then. "My phone just died. How much battery do you guys have left?"

"Mine is almost done too," replied Dwayne.

"Mine too," said Jason.

"I have a bit of battery left," I told them. "Let's call 911!"

Jason dialed 911. "Damn, I've got no signal," he reported.

"Neither do I," Dwayne confirmed.

"Same here," I said.

"That's weird," Jason remarked. "We had signal before. You don't think he's jamming us somehow, do you?"

"I bet he is," Dwayne concluded. "If he has cameras all over the place that we didn't see, he probably has a jammer too. The community college uses them to keep students off their phones during lectures."

"First we need to hide, like Michael said." I instructed. "Then we need to come up with a plan. Maybe we should turn on all the lights, then someone from the outside might see them and come check it out."

"Won't that make us easier to see?" asked Tia.

"Maybe, but he can already see us, so what's the difference?" I replied. "Michael, where should we hide?" But Michael had disappeared. "Michael? Where did you go?"

"He's gone," Jason said. "Let's go to the kitchen. Maybe we can find something to use as a weapon."

We moved as one, slowly walking single file towards the kitchen. Along the way we found the light switch. At least we didn't need to waste the last of our phone batteries.

A search of the kitchen turned up a single cake knife. Jason found a large serving fork and tucked a couple of butter knives into his pockets. I took the handle off the push broom. At least it was something. Besides, I had taken a self-defence course once, and they had taught me how to use a stick as a weapon. Anna and Tia were the only two still unarmed. A coffee pot likely wouldn't do.

Michael appeared once again. "He's almost here. You need to hide." He pleaded. "Please, I need you to hide. You can't beat him, he's too strong. The last couple thought they could beat him, and . . . ," he hung his head, "and they were wrong."

"Okay," Jason said. "Let's go upstairs. We can hide in the offices. I noticed the two at the front were connected, so we can hide in one and have two escape routes. We'll turn on all the lights along the way."

Jason started for the stairs at front of the funeral home. We flipped on the all the lights as we went: the hall, the family room and clergy room, even the bathrooms. Dwayne and Tia ran to get the reception area and the office.

We all scrambled up the stairs, flipping lights on in the hall and then in each room we passed. I felt a little better with the lights on. Jason led us into the room on the right and we all moved towards the desk.

"We need to barricade!" Dwayne cried.

Anna and I overturned the desk while Tia pulled drawers from the filing cabinet, making it light enough for the guys to move it into place. In two minutes we had a barricade in a corner of the room, with a small opening on each end. We settled in and waited.

"I see you found the light switches," the voice said over the intercom system. "While I admire the thought, I think I'll turn the tide in my favour. I do hope your phones are all well charged."

Suddenly the light in the room across the hall went out. Then the hall. Dwayne crept to the door and reported that all the lights downstairs were now out. The only light left was in our room. And then, we were plunged into darkness. Dwayne's phone blinked on as he made his way behind the desk. "What do we do now? He knows this place like the back of his hand. He's just playing with us. He sees our every move."

"I think we make a stand right here," Jason proposed. "At least we know he has to come at us from one of two doors and then around the barricade. Tia and Anna hide in the bathroom. Beth, Dwayne and I will try and tackle him or something if he comes in here."

I nodded in agreement and Tia and Anna went to the bathroom. We closed the door and waited in the dark.

"Allee, allee, all come free." The voice was close enough that he didn't need to use the speakers. "I wonder where you're hiding. Oh, that's right, you went upstairs. I hope you're ready. This little game of hide-and-seek won't last too long."

He made a show of stomping up the stairs. "Are you in here? Nope." A door closed. "How about here? Nothing again!" Another door slammed shut. "Now, I know where you are." Conor almost sang the words.

My skin crawled. I heard another door, and footsteps coming even closer.

"Oops, wrong room. That means you're over here!" Conor sounded almost excited. "BOO!"

A rectangle of light framed a silhouette as the door to our room opened. The next thing I heard was Jason's voice. "Get him Dwayne!" And then some *splat* sounds. We all rushed around our barricade. We scuffled, crowding the silhouette back out the door, and I managed to get a few licks in. His footsteps thumped away, and then, just silence. We stood there for a moment, listening for him before opening the bathroom door.

"It's ok. He's gone." It was Dwayne.

Tia jumped up and ran to him, jumping into his arms. "I was so scared! What happened? Where is he?"

Just then Jason appeared behind him with his phone's flashlight on. "It was the funeral director. He was just playing with us. He opened the door and just stood there for a minute. Then he threw water balloons at us."

That's when I noticed that we were all wet. But it didn't look like water. "Uh guys, I don't think it was water in those balloons!" I shone my phone on us, and that's when we all noticed we were dripping with red liquid. "Is that . . ."

"BLOOD" we all screamed at once.

Jason slowly raised his arm and smelled the red liquid. Then, to my surprise, he licked it and smiled. "Just strawberry syrup."

Anna moved around me and ran to Jason. They embraced. "I'm so glad you're ok, baby," she said, giving him a long kiss on the lips. She didn't seem to mind getting the sticky syrup all over her.

"What was all the noise?" Anna asked.

"We chased him," replied Jason, "but he was fast. He was halfway down the stairs before we even got out of the room. By the time we were at the bottom he was gone. I don't think staying in one place is going to work. Who knows what he'll throw at us or do the next time? We were sitting ducks."

Just then we heard Conor's voice over the speakers. "Wasn't that fun? You see, you aren't safe anywhere. This will be a fun night, filled with adventure. What comes next? Only I know. But for now, know that I'm watching your every move and that I will prevail. None of you will ever leave my house." He laughed and then all went silent again.

"I'm going to try to call the police again," I said. "Maybe up here near a window I can get a signal. I moved to the window and turned my phone back on. When it came up, I didn't see any bars but tried to call anyway, holding it right against the window. Nothing. "Rats! I was hoping that maybe we were far enough away from whatever is blocking the signal. Maybe in the church?"

"Good idea," said Dwayne. "Maybe, if we somehow got up into the bell tower, we could get a signal. We just have to figure out how to sneak back there without being seen."

CHAPTER 22

WE STAYED IN the upstairs office for a few minutes to catch our breath and come up with a plan. Jason was pacing back and forth. Dwayne and Tia whispered quietly enough that I couldn't hear, and Anna just sat in a chair, watching Jason.

"OK, any ideas?" I asked after about five minutes. "My first thought is to stay together and cautiously walk back the way we came. If he saw Dwayne take a mint, he must be watching us through cameras anyway. If we are together, what can he do? We're five and he's just one."

"One that knows his way around much better than we do," Jason said. "And if he has cameras, he'll know our every step. We don't even know if he's armed, but I think we should assume he is. How much battery power do we each have?"

"I have about twenty-five percent," I said.

Dwayne responded with "Ten."

"And I have twenty-two," Jason continued. "We can't use the phones for light anymore unless it's absolutely necessary."

"I don't think we should split up," I asserted. "Haven't you ever watched a horror movie? When you split up, it makes it easier for the killer to get you."

"I'm with Beth," agreed Dwayne. "No one goes off by themselves, for anything, under any circumstances. Agreed?"

We all nodded.

We took a minute to gather our courage, and then we went to the door. Jason and Anna went first, Jason stopping for a moment to open the door and peer out. Seeing nothing, he led us out. Dwayne followed Anna, then Tia and me. I'm not sure how I ended up last, but it was definitely not the place I felt safest. I was terrified as we made our way out of the office.

We crept slowly down the hall to the top of the stairs, not using our phones for light. Each creek of the floor sent my skin crawling, and I constantly looked behind me. I kept thinking that someone was right behind me, ready to pounce. I had to force myself to breathe. I was surprised my heart beat on its own. The two or three minutes it took us to creep to the top of the stairs felt like an eternity. My mind kept racing. *What if we die?* I thought. *Stop thinking like that*, I told myself. But I had so many questions for which I had no answers. *Who is this guy? Why is he terrorizing us? Why did I let myself get talked into breaking in? Will we ever make it out of here?*

I was so caught up in my thoughts I almost ran into Tia, barely noticing that the group had stopped at the top of the stairs.

"He's watching you." I jumped and turned to see Michael standing behind me.

"Dang it!" I whispered. The others turned to look. "You scared me, Michael."

"Sorry." He paused. "He's watching you. He knows you're trying to get downstairs. He sees you on his phone. I don't know what he's planning, but he's angry and happy at the same time. I can feel it. You need to find a way out."

"We're trying." I said. "Do you know where he is?"

"He's downstairs, in the room with all the knives," Michael told us.

"That's great!" whispered Dwayne. "We can go straight to the chapel if he's in the kitchen. We can get by him. Jason, let's try the front door and then sneak right down the hall and around to the chapel. We won't go near the kitchen."

"Sounds good," replied Jason. "Change of plans. We try the front door and if we can't get it open, we head straight to the chapel." We all nodded in agreement. I turned back to Michael, but he was already gone.

With renewed hope and a new plan, we slowly made our way down the stairs, single file, keeping to the edges to reduce the risk of squeaks. "I know he can see us, but no sense in giving him audio too. Maybe we'll catch him not watching his phone," Jason suggested.

At the bottom of the stairs, we crept around the display of cards and peeked into the office. Empty. Good. We hurried past and went through the first set of doors, closing them quietly behind us. Jason tried the entry door. It didn't budge. He turned the deadbolt and tried again. Nothing. Dwayne quietly moved past Anna and joined Jason at the door, and they pushed it with their shoulders. I could see the muscles on their necks and backs strain beneath their shirts. No movement. They readjusted for more leverage and pushed again. They strained with all they had for about thirty seconds. I leaned in and got a piece of the door as well. Still nothing.

"Well, I guess that's our answer," Dwayne said. "Either I've lost all my strength, or it's sealed closed somehow."

Jason nodded. "Let's get moving, then. Single file and quiet again. I'll go first." He opened the inner door and looked around, and then moved through it. I reached out and caught it, holding it open for everyone before slipping through myself, closing it quietly behind me. I took a little too long to close it, and found myself thirty feet behind the rest of the group. No one seemed to notice. I didn't want to risk making noise, so I kept moving slowly, figuring they would stop before going through the next door to pass the morgue, and I could catch up with them then.

But I was moving more slowly than the rest. I kept stopping to listen and make sure no one was following me. I ended up far enough behind that when I rounded the corner, Dwayne and Tia were already going through the next door. Tia turned and nodded to me like they had been waiting for me to come around the corner. I could see Jason and Anna going into the chapel through the door at the other end. All was going well.

The door closed just before I reached it. I took in a whiff of that sweet cherry smell from the morgue. *Funny, I thought, we didn't smell that in the hall before, only in the morgue.* I turned the handle, but it wouldn't open. I looked through the window and knocked. Tia and Dwayne stopped and turned around. Tia said something to Dwayne and started my way. That's when I saw the door to the morgue open. I screamed at Tia, who stopped and turned around. I furiously shook the door but it wouldn't budge. I banged for Tia to come open it, but she just stood there. Like a statue.

CHAPTER 23

I WATCHED IN HORROR as the scene before me unfolded in slow motion.

From the door of the morgue Conor O'Reagan flew into the room. He ran full force with his elbows up, connecting with Dwayne's face just as he turned around. Dwayne had no time to react, and his face took the full force of Conor's attack. His head bounced off the wall behind him and he dropped to the floor.

As he struggled to pick himself up, Conor kicked him in the stomach and legs, keeping him down. Tia finally moved. Instead of running towards me and the relative safety of the funeral home, she ran straight at Conor. She let out a blood-curdling scream as she launched herself through the air, attempting to jump on Conor's back. But her scream gave Conor enough of a warning to turn and see her, and he put up his hands and blocked her. She fell to the floor, but not before her right foot caught Conor squarely between the legs. Conor let out a yelp and bent over slightly, catching his breath.

"No!" I cried, "Tia, get up! Get up!"

Tia scrambled to her feet and faced Conor, who smiled. I heard him say, "You should have stayed back. Now, I guess it's your turn instead of —" Dwayne, back on his feet, threw himself at Conor, tackling him around the waist and driving him to the floor.

"Yes!" I screamed through the door.

Dwayne was on top of Conor, who was face down. Dwayne's face was bloodied. His nose didn't look right, and he was missing a front tooth. Blood dripped from his chin, down onto the back of Conor's head.

I could see Jason at the far end of the hall, trying frantically to open his door. Neither of us could get through. We were helpless.

Dwayne started punching Conor in the back of the head. Conor swung an elbow and caught Dwayne in the temple, stunning him. Conor twisted beneath him. Another punch caught Dwayne squarely in the nose. He yelped in pain. I could see blood fly as a fist smashed flat his already broken nose. Conor made a quick move with his feet and pulled Dwayne over backwards and landed on top. Tia, on her feet again, ran at Conor and jumped on his back, hammering at the top of his head with her fists.

"Yes! Get him Tia!" I called.

Conor reached back with one hand and grabbed her by the hair. He pulled her over his shoulder, and she landed on Dwayne with a thud I could feel through the floor.

Still holding her hair, Conor stood and dragged Tia down the hall in my direction, all the time smiling and staring straight at me. I just stared back. I noticed I was crying. He got to the door and held Tia up by one hand and then simply dropped her to the floor.

"It's not her turn," was all he said as he turned and walked back to Dwayne.

Dwayne had made it to his knees. He had a flat, bloody mess where his nose used to be. Blood flowed from it — down, into, and around his lips — and continued to drip from his chin, pooling on the tile floor. His right eye had swollen shut. He tried to stand as Conor approached him, but Conor simply tapped him on the forehead as he walked by, knocking him back to the floor like a ragdoll.

I could hear Tia weeping at the foot of my door. I could hear her as she weakly knocked on it. She was sobbing, begging me to help, not realizing I was helplessly locked behind it. "Dwayne," she called, over and over. "Dwayne, get up." But he never moved.

I looked up again to see Conor at the far door. He lifted his right hand and waved it in front of Jason's face, mocking him. Then he pointed at him and drew his left hand across his throat. He threw his head back and laughed. His laugh sent a ripple down my spine. His backside was covered in Dwayne's blood. I couldn't believe how much blood there was.

Conor turned, still laughing, and walked back to Dwayne, who lay motionless, one leg tucked under him. Conor had a welt over his left eye where Dwayne must have caught him with a punch.

The mortician bent down and grabbed Dwayne by the wrist and dragged him towards the morgue door. "NOOO!" I heard Tia scream. Then she was on her feet running at him once more. He looked up and smiled, dropping Dwayne's arm. He took a step towards Tia to meet her with a big backhand that sent her flying. The sound was horrible, even through the door. Tia lay on the floor, motionless.

Conor turned back to Dwayne, grabbed his wrist once more and pulled him into the morgue. The door closed behind him. I looked down the hall, where Jason and Anna stared back at me. Both doors remained locked.

I turned and slid down the door to the floor. I dropped my head and began to sob.

"Beth," I heard. "Beth. You need to get up." It was Michael. "You need to get up. Follow me. I'll show you how to see him. I know where he watches people."

I looked up. "Michael? Why didn't you save him? Why didn't you help me save him?"

"I couldn't. I can't stop him, he's too strong, but I'm trying to help you. Maybe I can save you and help you save them." He began to walk back the way I had come. I slowly stood and turned back to the door. I tried it again and it still wouldn't open. But Tia was moving. Thank God she wasn't dead. I slapped on the door to get her attention.

"Get up, Tia!" I yelled through the door. "Get up!"

I turned back to see Michael standing there, waiting.

I could hear the muffled screams of Jason and Anna from the other end of the hall. I could see their fists banging on their door, when it suddenly opened. They ran into the hall. Anna stopped at Tia while Jason ran to the door of the morgue, trying desperately to get in and save Dwayne, but the door wouldn't open. Then he ran up to my door. He pushed while I pulled.

"Hide!" Jason urged. "We'll find a way to get to you. We'll get Tia and make a plan to come back and get you. Just hide." I put my hand on the glass like in a cheesy movie, and he did the same.

"I love you," I mouthed, and then turned away as tears and snot flowed freely down my cheeks. I wiped at my nose with the back of my hand. I walked towards Michael.

The boy turned and led me back upstairs. I turned my flashlight app on to go up the stairs. The last thing I wanted was to trip and fall. I wasn't really paying attention to where we were going and was surprised when I found we had gone to Conor's office. "There," Michael said, pointing to the computer screen. "The man watches people on that." And then he was gone. He just faded into nothing.

"Michael?" I called. No answer. I sighed and sat in Conor's desk chair. I reviewed the events of the past few minutes in my head. If only I had hurried to stay with the group, then there would have been three against one. I needed to figure out how to get back with my friends. Being alone in the dark with a psychopath looking for me was not a good plan.

I touched the mouse. The computer screen jumped to life, and I saw feeds from the cameras around the funeral home. I looked closely at each box on the screen. I could see the front entry of the house in one box, the room with all the furniture in another, the hall where Dwayne was attacked in another. The fourth box held a feed from the kitchen, and the last showed the reception room. I clicked on an arrow on the right of the screen and scrolled to another five cameras. In the first box I could see Jason, Anna, and Tia. They were huddled in the front of the chapel. Anna was tending to Tia's wounds and hugging her. I could tell that Tia was sobbing. Jason was pacing back and forth.

As I watched them, movement caught my eye in another screen. It was the morgue. Of course — the knives Michael had talked about were the scalpels! Conor had Dwayne on one of the metal tables. His clothes were off, and he wasn't moving.

Conor had a lab coat and gloves on. I watched as he gently wiped the blood from Dwayne's face and hair with a sponge. He rinsed the rest of Dwayne's body, gently wiping down his skin. When he was finished washing, Conor patted him dry with a towel and then began to re-dress him. It looked like Conor was talking to Dwayne as he did this. He even combed Dwayne's hair.

Then he went to another table, but it wasn't a table at all. It was a casket on wheels. He pushed it over next to the table, tight up against one side. I couldn't stop watching as Conor reached across and grabbed Dwayne's ankles, pulling them into the casket, followed by his hips and then his body. In less than a minute, he had moved Dwayne from the table into the casket.

I saw Dwayne move.

He lifted his hand to his head. Conor took it and put it back down at Dwayne's side and appeared to say something to him. Then Conor placed a cover over the lower half of Dwayne's body. He took a drill and began to screw the lid on. Dwayne appeared to be waking now, and I saw the lid bump up, but Conor kept on screwing it down. One of Dwayne's arms came out from under the lid and grasped at Conor, who kept on working. Then Dwayne had hold of Conor by the lab coat, and he yanked hard. Conor stumbled and dropped the drill. He bent to get it, and when he stood up, he was met by an elbow from Dwayne. *Good shot!* I thought.

The resistance was short lived, however, as Conor hit Dwayne in the forehead with the butt of the drill. Dwayne's arms went limp, and Conor tucked them back under the lid.

He finished securing the lid on the lower part of the casket and then added the upper piece, over his head. Once it was screwed down, he pushed the casket to the far side of the morgue, to the door of the crematorium. That's when it hit me. Conor was going to cremate Dwayne alive!

Immediately I was screaming inside — or was it a real scream? "NO!" It must have been out loud because suddenly Conor stopped and looked at the camera. He smiled and gave a slight wave and then went to the door and opened it, pushing through it the casket that held Dwayne. Then the door closed.

I found them on another camera. Conor was positioning another trolley up to the end of the casket. Conor adjusted its height, making it level with the other table, and then pushed Dwayne onto it. There were rollers on the top of the new trolley, so the casket moved easily. Then he moved Dwayne to the door of what I realized was the furnace.

Conor went around the end of the furnace and typed something into a keyboard and came back. He pushed a button beside the furnace door, and it opened. He went to the back of the casket and pushed Dwayne into the cremation chamber.

As Conor closed the chamber door, I told myself, *Think Beth, there has to be a way you can help.* And then it came to me. There was another door off the kitchen into the garage, and a door from the garage to the morgue. Maybe I could get in.

I jumped up from my chair and ran to the door, tripping on the edge of the desk as I hurried. Right, flashlight. I turned on the app and bounded down the stairs. I wasn't thinking about the noise, I was just trying to save Dwayne.

At bottom of the stairs, I could hear Dwayne screaming. I ran faster.

Down the hall to the kitchen. I burst through the door to the garage and ran straight into the hearse with a thud, falling to the floor. I got to my feet. Had I been thinking, I might have been surprised to find the door to the morgue open, but it was, and I ran right through. I took a quick look for Conor and saw nothing — but there was that smell again. I went to the door marked Crematorium and went in. I pushed the button that Conor had to raise and lower the door.

I hadn't yet realized that there were no more screams.

As the door came up, I saw the flames. So many flames. That's when I noticed the silence. It was so hot. I could barely look through the door, even from a bit of distance. The whole casket was burning. I looked for something to pull it out with, but there was nothing big enough, just a few long-handled brushes. As the casket fell away, I saw Dwayne's corpse, engulfed in flames. There were no more movements, no more screams, just burning flesh and bones.

I sank to the floor, sobbing. I thought of Dwayne and our friendship. We had met in fourth grade at Park Street Elementary. Mrs. Wilson had been our teacher. Dwayne had just moved to town with his family, and we became fast friends and had stayed friends ever since. I'd known him longer than I had Jason or Anna. Then I thought of Tia. Oh Tia! I had to get to the others. I had to figure out how I was going to get past Conor and rejoin them. But wait, I was almost there! I ran from the crematorium and headed for the door to the hallway. It opened and I burst through, heading for the chapel. I froze in my tracks.

CHAPTER 24

"HELLO, DEAR. IN the mood for a barbeque?" He was leaning against the door at the other end of the hall. The dim lights from the parking lot on the other side of the translucent windows gave him an even more sinister look.

"I do hope you and your friends have learned your lesson. You see, it's not polite to break into someone's home. I think you will find the punishment is quite severe."

"You sick bastard!" I screamed. "Why did you have to kill him? He didn't deserve to die. We didn't break anything or hurt anything. We just wanted to see the ghost." I was finding some strength in my rage. "When we get out of here, you're going to jail!"

"My dear, haven't you figured it out yet? None of you are leaving here. I have plans for each and every one of you. I do like your spirit though. Perhaps I should leave you for last." He took a step towards me and then another, as he spoke. I held my ground, partly out of defiance but mostly because I was frozen in terror.

"We will get out. We are stronger than you know," I challenged. "Besides, it's four against one. When I get back to my friends, we'll find a way out, and then the police will know everything. Michael will help us."

"Michael, that little annoyance. He's nothing more than snivelling child. He can't do anything to help. As for the police — please. 'Officer, I woke up this morning to find my funeral home a mess. The cremation chamber was turned on, and something was burned in there, and I found this girl, covered in blood, kneeling at the altar, confessing she had just killed someone. I'm not sure what that's all about, but I captured her. She's quite strong. As you can see, she left me with a few cuts and bruises.'" He mocked. "Who do you think the sheriff will believe? His old school friend or a stranger, who I have on video, breaking into my property?"

He took two more quick steps towards me, and I jumped back, turned, and ran towards the chapel. I could hear him laughing behind me as I pushed through the door. As I tumbled in, I ran face first into Jason, bounced off him, and landed hard on the floor. Jason jumped back and looked like he was ready to fight.

"Beth!" he cried. "Oh Beth, we thought we'd never see you again. Are you Okay? Did he hurt you?"

"We need to go!" I yelled. "He's right behind me. We need to hide!" I jumped up and ran for the back stairwell where we had entered. I turned on my flashlight app as I flew the few yards to the stairs. I turned to make sure everyone was following, then plunged into the darkness below, heading for the basement and whatever we would find there. After the last step I burst through a door into a wide, open space. Thank God the door wasn't locked, I thought, or I'd have likely broken a bone. I looked around using my phone light and could see several doors, which I assumed led to classrooms. At the far end was a pair of doors on either side of a large pass-through window. That must be the kitchen, I thought.

"Follow me!" I said, as I ran for the door on the right. It opened into the old church kitchen. I finally allowed myself to stop. I leaned on the kitchen island and tried to catch my breath. Jason, Anna, and Tia all followed me in.

"Did he follow us?" I asked.

Jason went to the door and peered out, using his phone to scan the room. "Nothing," he reported. "It's all quiet. I don't think he's chasing us."

That's when I completely fell apart. I dropped to the floor sobbing. The events of the past few minutes raced through my mind. I saw the fight with Tia. Dwayne, beaten and dragged away. I saw Jason coming through the door to Tia. I relived not being able to help. I saw Dwayne being thrown into the cremation chamber. I heard his screams again. I remembered being too late to save him. The pain I felt burst forth.

Anna, then Tia, joined me on the floor. They held me, rocked me, soothed me. All the while, Jason kept watch out the door. Nobody said a word. The only sound in the room, in the whole basement, was me, sobbing.

After several minutes, Tia asked, "Where's Dwayne?"

I looked up at her with my tear-stained face. "He's . . . he's dead," I sobbed. "I tried to save him, but I couldn't. I got to him too late. Conor cremated him . . . alive. I'm so sorry. I tried to save him, but . . ." That was as far as I could get before I broke down again. I felt Tia get up. She screamed. It was a terrible scream. One that made my insides quiver. I looked up and saw fury on her face. There wasn't a tear.

There was no fear. In that moment, she was simply blood-red angry.

"Conor!" She screamed again, at the top of her lungs. There was so much rage in that scream it made me shudder.

Before he could stop her, Tia ran past Jason and out into the big room. He glanced back at me and Anna. "Stay here!" he ordered, and then he went after her.

We huddled together behind the island, waiting. We heard the far door to the stairs open once, then twice. We heard two sets of footsteps on the floor above, just a second or two apart. Then we heard a muffled scream and a lot of banging. I had no idea if Conor had ambushed them or if they were fighting with each other or if Tia was just throwing a fit.

"Do you think he got them?" asked Anna. "It sounds like he attacked them."

"I don't know," I replied. "I hope not, but we better be ready, just in case. Look around and see if we can find something to use as a weapon."

We opened drawers and doors, looking for something, anything, we could use to defend ourselves. We found paper plates and cups, punch bowls and ladles, napkins — lots of napkins — plastic cutlery, and aprons. Not a lot to fight with.

"I got my weapon!" Anna beamed as she pulled a big wooden rolling pin out of a drawer. "It should work well, it's nice and heavy." She swung it a couple of times with a wicked grin.

"Help me find something?" I asked. "Hurry. I don't hear anything anymore."

"He could be coming!" Anna exclaimed.

I opened another drawer just as we heard the far door to the stairs close, more quietly than it had a few minutes before. Inside, I found one of those big forks that's used for roasts. Anna hid behind the door with the rolling pin raised. I ducked behind the far end of the island, ready to attack.

A quiet knock on the door. "Anna? Beth? It's us." It was Tia. The door opened and she and Jason walked through. Anna jumped out from behind the door, dropping the rolling pin. Jason and Tia both jumped.

"You almost gave me a heart attack," Tia said.

Anna jumped on Jason, wrapping her arms around his neck, planting a kiss on his lips. Jason wrapped his arms around her and returned the kiss before setting her down.

"What was all the noise?" I asked.

"Tia was like a crazy woman," Jason smiled. "She was running so fast I couldn't keep up. Then when the door to the funeral home wouldn't open, she started screaming and banging. I thought for sure Conor was going to come after her, but we didn't see anything. All the lights are still off, and both of our phones are now dead, so we couldn't see much if we wanted too. That reminds me, how much battery do you have left, Beth?"

I took out my phone. "Eighteen percent," I told him. "Not much, but if I don't use it for a flashlight, I've got enough for a couple of hours."

"OK. Save it for a chance to make a call," he told me. "We need to find a spot where we can get a signal. Did anyone try the phones here in the church? Maybe they still have old school land lines. Then he can't jam the signal." He lifted the receiver of the phone on the kitchen wall, then slammed it back down, causing the receiver to bounce off the cradle and fall to the floor. "Damn!" he yelled.

Then the speaker system crackled to life.

CHAPTER 25

"SO HOW ARE we all doing?" cackled Conor. "Are you enjoying your little adventure so far? It's such a shame that blondie couldn't save the big guy. If only she had been a few minutes faster. Oh wait, then she would have had to get by me. And little one, I take it he held a special place in your heart? I'm so sorry you lost him, but you'll be joining him soon enough. Now, who's next? Should I rid myself of the boys first or go boy–girl?"

We all looked at each other. "Can he see us?" I whispered.

"What's that, dear? It's too dark to read those pretty little lips of yours. If you're wondering what I've decided, you'll simply have to wait and see. You'll discover I have something special planned for each of you. I'm not so sure you'll like it as much as I will. You see, I've always been told that practice makes perfect, so I intend to practice something I don't get to do very often. It should help me in my future endeavours. Now, you guys may want to move, because I'll be down to the kitchen in a few minutes. I've unlocked the doors once again, so feel free to roam about. You should also take the weapons you found. It'll make it more fun for me. What is that, a rolling pin, dear? Again, it's a little hard to tell in the dark, even with the night vision camera.

"Oh yes, all the phones are out and will remain that way throughout the evening. I wouldn't want anyone spoiling my fun with a call to the police. Although, a 911 call would simply get you through to Sheriff Johnson, and I'm not sure he'd be much help. Enjoy the rest of your tour. I'm afraid your time is ticking away."

We heard the crackle of the speakers as he turned them off.

No one moved. I'm not sure anyone even breathed for a long time. Too long. "We have to move," I said with authority. "Everyone up. Move! He's coming."

"I've been thinking. What if he just wants us to think he's coming when really, he's hoping we move. He could be hiding somewhere, just waiting for us to come to him," Jason pondered. That's when we heard footsteps above us, heading for the back stairs that led down to the basement, and to us.

"He's coming!" I almost yelled.

"The front stairs," Anna directed. "They go up to the entrance where the bell tower is."

We moved as one chaotic organism, almost tripping over each other with every step. Anna tripped on the first step, fell, and Tia landed on top of her. They scrambled to get up and we heard Conor again. Close this time. There was no need for the speaker system.

"Allee, allee, all come free," he almost sang. "Where are those church mice running off too? I bet I know — up the front stairs! You better run, or it will be too late." His laugh scared me more than anything else he did.

I pushed the group from behind, almost knocking Jason over and starting a domino chain. Luckily, he caught his balance and averted disaster. We got to the top, and Anna led the way down the side hall along the outside of the main auditorium. She scurried around behind the stage, and we all jumped into the baptismal and ducked down. We sat there gasping, trying to breathe.

"Where are you?" rang the voice. "I know you came up here. Are you under the pews? No. In the other stairwell?" We listened as he walked across the stage, pausing next to the curtain that hid the baptismal tank. We all held our breath, expecting Conor to pull the curtains aside and discover us. Then, after a moment, he moved on, opening the door to the stairwell.

"Hello? Anyone down there? Did you all circle back?" he called down the stairs.

Then we heard him move to the door that led to the funeral home. We heard it open, then a few footsteps, and then it closed. No one moved. We hardly breathed. We sat there for at least fifteen minutes. It got hot and sticky. Finally, when we couldn't bear it any longer, Jason slowly stood. He pulled the curtain back a little and peeked out. Then he poked his head out and looked around completely. "He's gone," he said.

All at once, everyone let out a breath. One by one we stood and stretched. For a moment we relaxed. My heart finally stopped racing. *The office*, I thought. *We can see where he is.*

"I have an idea," I said. "Up in his office, there is a computer that shows all the cameras. If we can see him, maybe we can figure out how to get out of here. Maybe he'll lead us to the controls for the locks or something. Either way, at least we'll know where he is."

"Good idea," replied Jason. "Lead the way."

I climbed out of the baptismal tank and headed cautiously for the door Conor had used a few minutes before. It opened and we slowly made our way along the hallway past the morgue, pausing to listen at the door.

Conor was singing:

"Five blind mice.

Five blind mice.

See how they run,

I'm having fun.

The Funeral Directors gonna chase,

The little mice are all locked in place,

Five blind mice.

Five dead mice."

We looked at each other in horror. He knew we were outside the door.

"Don't worry," Conor called. "I'm not ready for you yet. 'I'm going to prepare a place for you. When everything is ready, I will come get you.'" I recognized the scripture reference from the Bible. John, Chapter 14, I thought. Then he started to sing again.

"Fast!" I hissed. And we all ran through the next door into the funeral home, around the corner and up the stairs. We didn't stop until we got to the office. That's when I noticed Tia wasn't with us. "Tia!" I exclaimed. "Where is Tia?"

"Wait here," Jason said, and then he was gone, racing out the door and down the stairs.

"Here," I said to Anna as I wiggled the mouse, bringing the computer screen to life. We scanned the cameras until we saw Jason running towards the door to the morgue. We watched as he ran into it, found it locked, and fell to the floor from the impact. He picked himself up and tried over and over again to get through. We could hear his muffled screams as they made their way through the funeral home and up the stairs. Anna began to weep and collapsed on the floor.

I switched between screens frantically, back and forth, trying to find Tia, thinking only of finding her and not of what I might actually see. And then, there she was. On a table in the morgue. How did he get her? He said he wasn't ready for us! How on earth did we not notice until it was too late? But — where was Conor? I couldn't see him. I began to panic. Jason, where was Jason? Shouldn't he be back by now?

I kept flipping between the camera screens, and suddenly Jason came through the door.

"I couldn't save her." He was crying.

Anna got up off the floor, still crying herself, and they embraced. "I know," she said.

They must have noticed I was fixed on the screen. "What are you doing?" Jason asked.

"Trying to find Conor. He isn't in the morgue with Tia," I replied. "I can't find him anywhere. There must be a few blind spots in the camera coverage, or maybe he has a secret room or something."

I went back to the view of the morgue. Tia was still on the table, but she was moving now. "Tia's still alive!" I yelled. "Come here, look."

"We have to get to her. We have to save her," whispered Anna. "We can't lose her too."

"I don't know where Conor is," I said. "We could be running right into a trap. What if he's using her as bait?"

"We have to try. Try and find Conor again. Maybe we can see him. If he's far enough away, maybe I can get to her," Jason offered.

I searched for Conor and eventually went back to the morgue camera. There he was, eating a sandwich and staring up at the camera with a big smile.

"That bastard is just taunting us!" hissed Jason. "I'm going to kill him!" He ran from the room. I'd never seen him that angry.

"JASON, NO!" Anna chased after him. "He's just trying to bait you!" She was out the door.

I continued to watch Conor in case he moved. He didn't. He just stood there, leaning against the counter, looking up at the camera, eating and smiling.

Jason and Anna returned. "Is he still in the morgue?" Anna asked.

"Yes, he's still there. Just eating his sandwich," I responded.

"We need to plan. What if we split up and attack from both sides, one through the garage and one through hall?" Jason asked. "Maybe if one of us makes a move from one side, we can distract him long enough to save her."

"You forget the door is locked, and we can't get to the hall." I pointed out. "But what if we set a fire? Maybe in the bathroom, just on our side of the door? He would have to come out through the hall and leave Tia unguarded, wouldn't he?"

"I think he would!" Jason said enthusiastically. "Beth, you're a genius!" He gave me a hug.

CHAPTER 26

I CHECKED THE MORGUE camera one last time. Conor was still there. He had his back to the screen and appeared to be looking through a drawer of instruments. "Hurry!" I said. "It looks like he's getting ready to do something. We need to save Tia!"

We all rushed from the office and crept quickly down the stairs.

"Check the desks in the front offices for a lighter or something." Jason directed. "I'll go down to the next room and look there."

Anna and I stuck together, not wanting to be alone. We checked both offices, then joined Jason in the hall near the restrooms. We had discovered nothing to help us start a fire.

"The kitchen," Anna suggested. "We always keep our matches and fire starters in a drawer in the kitchen."

We moved to the small kitchen and searched for a match or lighter. Nothing.

"The stove!" I said. "Turn on a burner and we can light a piece of paper or something."

We turned to the little stove. It was an induction burner. "It won't work. It only heats up metal," said Anna.

'OK, we need a new plan." Jason said. "Any ideas?"

When none of us could think of anything, Jason suggested we split up according to the first plan. Anna and I were to bang on the door in the hall while Jason attempted to sneak in through the garage. The hope was that Conor would simply come to the door and taunt us, giving Jason time to rescue Tia. We all prayed Conor wouldn't actually chase after us.

We agreed we would meet back up in the office whether it worked or not. We weren't to wait around for each other. Anna and I were to bang and scream for five minutes and then run. Jason would take a peek, and if the coast was clear, he would rescue Tia.

When we arrived at the door to the morgue, I pushed it to see if was unlocked. It opened. "Don't," whispered Anna. "What if it's a trap? He could be in there just waiting for us." Agreeing, I backed away and we ran for the garage, only to run right into Jason as we came into the kitchen. Anna was in the lead, so she actually ran into him and I ran into her. It was almost like a scene out of an old Scooby Doo! cartoon.

"Why didn't you guys make any noise?" Jason demanded. "I could have been caught."

"The door was open," Anna told him. "We thought it was a trap. We thought you were in danger."

"But what about Tia?" he asked.

"I think we should stick together and just take a look. Conor might be out trying to trap us, and Tia could be in there alone. We need to try," I said.

We looked at each other and without speaking a word, I led the way into the garage. As I neared the door to the morgue, I slowed. I felt my heartbeat speed up and for the first time I noticed I was sweating. I dried the palms of my hands on my shirt, put my hand on the doorknob, and pressed my ear to the door. I held my breath and listened. All I could hear was the sound of my heart beating in my ears. I turned the knob. I took a deep but quiet breath and gently pushed the door open an inch, then stopped to listen. Nothing. Two inches and I stopped again. I stuck my head through the door. *Lord, please don't let him be waiting on the other side with an axe or something*, I prayed.

I peered inside and didn't see Conor anywhere. I pushed the door open further, relaxing a little and stepped inside the morgue. Jason and Anna followed close behind.

That's when I saw her.

"Tia, oh, Tia!" I called, but she didn't move. I ran to the table she was lying on, stopped just short, and gasped. She was stark naked. Even her underwear had been removed, and her groin and breasts were barely covered by two small sheets. She was so white. I noticed a cut on her neck. There was tube sticking into one of her veins that was hooked up to some sort of machine. A small trail of blood ran down the length of the table. I reached out and touched her cheek. It was so cold. I checked for a pulse and found none. I jumped and screamed when Jason put his hand on my shoulder. I turned and buried my face in his chest. I wept uncontrollably. When I pulled myself away from him, I saw that he was holding Anna in his other arm. Everyone was in tears.

"I'm so sorry, Tia," I whispered.

"We were too slow. We should have come faster, and then she would still be alive." Anna said.

"No, if we had been faster, we'd likely all be dead already," Jason corrected. "I will kill this bastard if it's the last thing I do. Count on it."

Just then we heard a noise coming from the front hall. We froze.

"The Funeral Directors gonna chase,
The little mice are all locked in place,
Five blind mice. Five dead mice."

He was singing that song again!

"Out!" I hissed, "back through the garage."

We bolted as fast as we could while still keeping quiet. I took one look back as the garage door closed and saw a casket pushing its way through the door into the morgue. Conor looked up and we locked eyes. He smiled at me and nodded as the door closed. The exchange froze me in my tracks.

"Beth!" Anna startled me out of my trance. I turned quickly and ran after them.

We didn't stop until we got upstairs and into the office. Jason jumped into the chair behind the desk and wiggled the mouse, and the computer jumped to life.

We had left the camera showing a view of the morgue up on the screen. We watched in horror, huddled together, as Conor moved around Tia's lifeless body. He grabbed her legs and pulled them into the casket that he had moved up next to the table. Next, he guided her hips in and then gently cradled her head as her torso followed the rest of her body.

He placed her hands across her chest, then picked up a section of lid and used a drill to screw it down over her legs. He leaned down and kissed her on the forehead before putting the remaining cover section in place and securing it. Conor moved to one end of the casket and pushed her towards the crematorium door. I gasped. I knew what was next.

"He's going to cremate her." I whispered.

And then they were gone. They simply disappeared through the door. I didn't tell Jason and Anna there was a camera in the crematorium. I didn't want them to see what happened next. I couldn't bear to see it again myself.

We continued to watch in silence. After about ten minutes, Conor emerged from the crematorium, wiping his brow. He hung an apron on a hook outside the door and went to the sink to wash his hands. He was very deliberate, taking the same care as a surgeon on television. Scrubbing between each finger, washing all the way up to his elbows. Once he was finished with his hands, he washed his face and then dried himself off with a towel.

When he was finished, he picked up a pen and wrote something on a piece of paper. He turned and looked straight into the camera, holding the paper up so we could read the words: WHO'S NEXT?

Then Conor took out his phone and pushed a few buttons. He looked up at the camera, gave a smile and a wave, and then every camera feed on the screen went black. He had turned them all off. We could no longer track him.

CHAPTER 27

WE STARED AT the screen in silence. Finally, after about five minutes Jason spoke. "Well, what do we do now? How the hell do we beat him?"

Jason grabbed a coat tree and walked over to the lone window in the office. He hammered against the window until the wood splintered, and still not a single crack formed in the pane.

Anna and I looked at each other. Neither of us knew what to say. My head was spinning, trying to come up with an idea, any idea, on how get out of here. How were we to survive? I silently prayed, *Lord God we need help*. Then an idea came to me.

"What about the bell tower?" I asked. I'd forgotten about it. "If one of us could get up there and get high enough, maybe we could get a phone signal and call the police."

"That's a great idea!" Anna exclaimed. "Let's go!"

"Not so fast," cautioned Jason. "We need to be careful. We have no way to see where Conor is, but I bet he can still see us. It will take a miracle to get down that hall and past the morgue without getting caught. Any idea how to do that?"

"I do." We all jumped at the sound of Michael's voice. I had no idea when he'd showed up. None of us had noticed him until he spoke.

"Michael!" I exclaimed. "You scared me. When did you get here?"

"Just a few minutes ago. I was watching him and knew you'd need my help again. I can't stop him, but maybe I can help you," he told us.

"How?" Jason asked.

"I could watch him and tell you where he is. I could tell you when it's safe to go and warn you if he's coming," Michael explained.

"Where have you been all along?" Anna questioned. "We could have used your help to save Tia and Dwayne. Why help us now?"

"I don't know," Michael replied. "I'm not always . . . ," he paused, searching for words. "Here. Sometimes I'm somewhere else, and then I'm here again. I don't know how to explain it, but I'm back again, and I think I'm here for a while at least. I can't be sure, but I get the feeling I'm supposed to help you." He looked directly at me, but I assumed he meant he was to help all of us.

"Thanks, Michael. Can you help us get to the bell tower in the chapel? We want to try and call the police from up there. We're hoping the jamming device or whatever he's using won't reach up there."

"I think I can help you get there. Give me a minute to see where he is." Michael disappeared as quickly as he had appeared.

Jason looked at me and I shrugged.

After a minute, Michael appeared again. "He's still in the morgue. It looks like he's getting one of the tables set up for something. He's got a tray set up with some tools on it, beside one of the metal beds. He's whistling a song, too. I think he's very happy."

"That means we can at least get downstairs," I said.

"Let's get moving then," Jason agreed. "I'll go first."

Anna moved in behind him, so close she could have been riding on his back.

We moved slowly and quietly down the stairs. Jason led us into the front room without a word and took us around the door and into the corner. I looked behind me. Michael had followed.

"Can you see where he is now?" Michael disappeared without a word only to reappear a minute later.

"He's still in the morgue, but I think he's almost done. He's washing his hands," reported Michael.

"We need to move fast," Anna suggested. "Any ideas where to hide until he is away from the morgue and the hallway?"

"There were two stalls in the women's bathroom, and I don't think he'd put cameras in there. Would he?" I said.

"It's a chance we'll have to take." Jason responded. "Michael, can you keep an eye on him and warn us if he's heading our way before we get there?"

"Sure," and Michael disappeared once more.

"Let's go," Jason said.

Jason slowed at every door and took a quick peek inside each room we passed. We rounded the corner towards the morgue and then took a quick left towards the bathrooms. He stopped outside the women's bathroom before slowly opening the door and looking inside. It was windowless, pitch black.

"Can I see your phone, Beth?" He asked.

I unlocked it and handed it to him. "Careful, there isn't much battery left," I warned.

Jason turned on the flashlight app. He took a quick look and moved inside. "It's clear," he said.

He moved the garbage can to barricade the door and sat down up against it.

"Let's rest for a minute," he suggested. "Michael, can you go see where he is now?"

"OK," he replied.

"I'm turning off the phone," warned Jason. "It's going to get dark." We huddled close.

It felt like a long time before Michael returned. When he did, I noticed for the first time that there was a soft glow around him. A warm glow that was comforting and calming. It also allowed us to see each other, if only faintly.

"He's in the room with all the caskets. He's talking to himself about which casket he will pick for each of you. He can't make up his mind. I think he's going to be a few minutes."

"We should go," Anna said.

We slowly opened the door and made our way back towards the chapel. The door was open. We all collapsed on the front pew. The adrenaline pumping through my veins made me shake. I was exhausted, scared, and wired all at the same time.

CHAPTER 28

I DIDN'T SEE HOW anyone was going to get into the bell tower. There was a hatch leading up to it, covered with a piece of plywood. It looked like the access to our attic at home, only this one was ten feet up, maybe more.

"How are we going to get up there?" I asked. "The ceiling is a lot higher than normal."

"And *who's* going up there? I don't want to. What if it's a trap? What if there are bats or something?" said Anna.

"It's OK, honey," Jason assured her. "You don't have to go up there if you don't want to. What do you think Beth? Will you go up?"

"How? I can't jump that high — I can't even reach from a chair."

"I'll boost you," Jason suggested. "I think if you stand on my shoulders, you'll be high enough to reach it."

"So, if I get up, do I just call 911?" I asked.

"No. Remember that cop that pulled us over? She gave me her card and said if we ever needed help, we should call her." He pulled out his wallet and extracted the police officer's card from it. He handed it to me.

Maine State Police. Trooper Alice Maxwell 207-555-5555, it read.

"Let's give it a try." I said. "If she doesn't answer, I'll call 911. With our luck, 911 would just reach Sheriff Johnson, and the way Conor talks, he's a friend. It might make things worse for us. No use trying it unless we have to."

Jason held his hands together at his waist and I stepped onto them. I got a leg over his shoulders and then a second. Anna tried to help by steadying me. Finally, I was sitting on Jason's shoulders. I tried to stand up but only succeeded in pushing his neck sideways with my hands and almost smothering him to death. We looked like a couple of clowns, I'm sure. This wasn't going to work.

I tried to get down and ended up falling backwards and landing on my back with a thud. My breath was knocked out of me.

"Beth, are you ok?" Anna was standing over me.

I moaned and nodded, still breathless and unable to talk. I slowly stood up. "Well, that didn't work. What if we use a chair? Maybe I can get up from the seat?"

We found a chair and placed it under the opening in the ceiling. Jason stood with his back to the chair, positioned so I could use the chair back as a step. Anna sat on the edge of the seat to keep the chair from tipping over. I carefully climbed up the makeshift steps, holding onto Jason's hands for balance. I stepped onto his shoulders while he held my knees.

I had to bend so I didn't hit my head on the ceiling. Reaching up, I pushed the plywood away from the hole and stuck my head in. My shoulders were even with the opening in the ceiling.

"Hold my feet and give me a boost," I said to Jason.

I grabbed the edge of the opening with both hands, and with Jason pushing on my feet, managed to pull myself up into the attic. I coughed and sneezed as I disturbed years of dust, and it billowed into the air. I moved to a sitting position and looked around. It was almost pitch black. The only light came from a small window above a set of narrow stairs that ran along the front wall of the bell tower. The space where the bell would normally ring gaped open like an eerie maw.

"There's a set of stairs. I'm going to try and go up. Maybe I'll get a signal up higher." I called down. "So far, I still have nothing."

"Be careful," Anna warned. "Don't fall through the ceiling. My dad did that once when he was in our attic."

"Michael, are you still around?" I asked, hoping he was. There was no response. "Is Michael down there with you?"

"I don't see him," replied Jason. "He must have disappeared while you were climbing into the tower."

I slowly crept across the ceiling, being careful to check each step before putting my weight down completely. As I got to the bottom step, I ran face first into a big spider's web. I let out a scream and frantically flailed my arms around my face and head, trying to remove the web. I felt something crawling in my hair. I screamed again and beat my hands on my head, hoping to either kill it or swipe it away.

"Beth! Are you Okay? Beth!" screamed Anna.

When I didn't immediately respond I heard Jason call, "Beth! Answer us!"

"I'm okay. Spider web. Hair. Freaked out. Gimme a sec," I managed.

I cautiously put my right foot on the first stair, then tested each one to ensure it would accept my weight. When I got to the top, there was enough light to see by, coming in through the small stained glass window. It was eerie with all the different colours.

"I'm at the top!" I called down. I looked at my phone and I had a single bar. "I have a signal! One bar! I'm going to try and call. Pray that my battery lasts."

I punched in the number for Trooper Alice, praying with each number that she would answer. It was almost four a.m. We had been locked in here for four hours. The phone rang. Once. Twice. Three times. "Please don't let it go to voice mail" I prayed. Four times. On the fifth ring I heard a sleepy voice.

"This better be good. Do you know what time it is?" the voice on the other end said.

"Hello!" I almost screamed in my excitement. "Is this Officer Alice Maxwell of the Maine police?"

"Yes, it is, who's this?" Alice responded.

"My name is Beth Springle. You pulled us over the other day for speeding. My friend Jason was driving, and he started crying and you gave him your card and said to call if we ever needed help. We need help! My two friends have been killed and Conor is trying to get us too. We're locked in the funeral home here in Harrington. Please come." I heard my phone beep telling me it was about to die. "My phone is about to die."

"Harrington? I'm forty-five minutes away. And why should I believe you? Why didn't you call 911? Are you kids playing a prank?" Alice asked.

"Please," I begged, "you have to believe me. My phone is going to die. He killed Dwyane and Tia and he's trying to get us too. We're locked in the —" I heard the click as the phone died. "UGH!" I screamed.

"Quiet!" It was Michael. "He's coming."

"Where did you come from? When did you get here?" I asked him.

"Please, be quiet. He's almost here." Michael warned again.

I scrambled down the narrow staircase, calling softly as I went. "Guys! Hide! Conor is coming!"

"What?" was the response I heard. Then Anna screamed.

I froze. "Oh God," I prayed. "Please let Alice believe me. Help me."

CHAPTER 29

"WELL, HELLO THERE, my friends." It was Conor. "I trust you're enjoying your stay in my little funhouse. Did you honestly think you could escape? No one has yet. Why is it that you young people always think festival weekend means you can do anything you want? Why do you think you're above the law? Well, guess what? Now you're in my house, and like the good book says, 'the wages of sin is death.' Now, which of you wants to be the next to meet their maker? You, big guy? Or maybe the sweet little thing hiding behind you?"

"You devil!" I heard Jason scream. "You leave Anna alone. Let's you and me go at it once and for all. Are you man enough to stand toe to toe with me instead of sneaking up and sucker punching us? Dwayne would have beat you in a fair fight, you coward. Come on, just you and me."

I was impressed with Jason's courage. He really did love Anna and was willing to risk his life for her, and for us.

"What a brave little man you are." Conor cackled. "I could have snuck up behind you and knocked your head off just now. You really need to pay closer attention. Speaking of which, where is your friend? By my count there should still be three of you. I know she didn't get out. No one ever leaves here without my permission."

"We got separated." Jason told him. "I'm not sure where she is, but when I kill you, the three of us are getting out of here, and everyone will know what really happened."

I started to cry as Jason lied to protect me. I needed to do something to help, but what? Maybe I could surprise Conor and jump on him from above.

"No." It was Michael. Just one word and I knew I couldn't do it. I knew Michael was right. Somehow, he knew what I was thinking. For some reason, he was trying to protect me, so I stopped and listened. I slid just a little closer to the trap door. If Conor looked up at the right angle, he might see me now. I got right down to the floor and didn't move again. I could see part of the little foyer from my vantage point, but no one was there. They must be right below me.

"Oh, I don't think *you* killing *me* is in the cards tonight. Know this though, my friend, you're next." Then I heard Conor laugh again and my skin crawled.

Suddenly Jason screamed. I heard what must have been Jason running headlong and tackling Conor. Some scuffling and grunting and groaning, and then they were in my line of sight. It looked like a hockey fight. Jason's shirt was up over his head, and he was flailing, trying to hit Conor, who just kept dodging his fists. Conor pulled what looked like a pipe or a stick out from behind his back and brought it down hard against Jason's shoulders. Jason grunted and fell to the floor.

"You bastard!" Anna screamed as she swung the rolling pin, hitting Conor's back. He stopped and slowly turned towards her. She lunged at him and clawed at his face and landed a kick to his groin. Conor swung his right fist and connected with her head, knocking her to the floor. She landed with a dull thud and a groan. I couldn't see her where she landed.

Jason got to his feet. "Run, Anna! Hide!"

Conor turned his attention back to him and snarled, "It's time to end you." He kicked Jason in the stomach, causing him to double over, then hit him on the head with the steel pipe. Jason fell to one knee, only to be kicked in the jaw. I watched as he crumpled to the floor, his face covered in blood. Conor paused to look around. I assumed it was to find Anna, but she must have escaped, as his focus returned to Jason. He punched him squarely on the nose just as he tried to rise. Jason was beaten.

Conor bent down, grasped him by the collar and dragged him from my view. The dragging sound grew fainter, and a few seconds later I heard a door close, no doubt the door to the hallway outside the morgue.

I was about to jump down through the hole when Michael warned, "Don't move, he's not gone."

I tensed up and edged slowly back, then lay flat on the floor. I could see a very small portion of the room below, which meant he likely wouldn't see me. I forced myself to take slow, shallow breaths.

"Is anyone still here?" I almost let out a scream at the sound of his voice, it startled me so badly. "Well, if you are, know that there will be no escape. I've taken steps to ensure that. By dawn, you will be nothing but a memory for your friends and family. You see, I need to practice my craft so that I don't make mistakes when it counts. And who better to practice on than the brats who break into my home!" His voice was getting louder as he spoke. Angrier. "Make no mistake little girl, you will not live to see the sun rise!"

I heard his footsteps as he walked away. Then I heard the door close again and felt the tension release from my body, just a little. I was sobbing again. "Michael, is he gone this time?" I asked.

"Yes, he's gone." Michael responded. "I'll keep an eye on him, if you want to find your friend."

I looked at my watch: four oh five. It had been fifteen minutes since my call, or my attempt at a call. How was it only fifteen minutes? I prayed Trooper Alice had believed me and was on her way. Maybe she'd even call in the cavalry. I had to focus. I needed to find Anna, and we needed to get out of here, or at least stay hidden until help came.

I lowered myself through the hatch and then let myself drop the last few feet to the floor, bending deep at the knee to lessen the noise. I looked around. The chair had been tossed over. There was a hole in the wall in one spot and a dent in another. There was a small puddle of blood on the floor where Jason had lain bleeding while the monster had hit him.

I went cautiously down the stairs towards the kitchen. I'd look for Anna here and then go up the back stairs to check behind the platform and in the baptismal tank.

"Anna," I whispered. "Anna, it's me, Beth. Where are you?" I listed for an answer and heard nothing.

I moved forward, coming to the kitchen door. "Anna," I whispered again. "Are you in there, Anna? Please be in here!"

Still no response. I went in and looked around, and there was no sign of her. I made my way through the open room beyond the kitchen, criss-crossing the floor, checking each of the six smaller rooms off to the sides. I went up the back stairs, hoping I would find her behind the stage.

At the top, I paused to listen. The door to the hall by the morgue was only a few feet away. If Conor was lying in wait, that would likely be where. Fear washed over me again. I wasn't sure I could move. I looked down at my watch again. Four twenty. Time was crawling along.

I took a deep breath and willed myself forward. I peeked into the sanctuary before heading behind the platform. It was empty. I crept behind the stage. "Anna," I paused. "Anna, are you back here?" No answer. The baptismal tank was empty too. I sighed. She must have gone back to the main funeral home. I would have to go past the morgue.

CHAPTER 30

I RETURNED TO THE sanctuary and took a seat on the front pew. The only passage to the funeral home was right outside the door. I didn't want to go. Conor would likely be in the morgue. As I walked down the hall, there would only be one wall between us. If he decided to take a peek out the door, or if he needed something in the storage room, I would be done for. Should I just hide somewhere and leave Anna on her own?

I don't know why, but I prayed again. "God help me to get past the psycho and get to the funeral home. Help me to be safe and to find Anna. Please keep her safe until I find her. And most of all, please bring help." I hadn't prayed in years, but it felt right to start again now.

I heard Michael say, "It's safe to go now. Conor is busy, so he won't be looking for you. Go now and you can get to the funeral home."

I nodded, stood up, and crept down the hall, then quietly slipped through the door on the other end. Once in the funeral home, I stopped and took a couple of deep breaths as I leaned against the wall. My muscles ached and I was exhausted, but I had to find Anna.

I checked both bathrooms, calling softly as I opened the doors and got no response. Then I tried the kitchen, hall, and casket room. I didn't dare look in the garage as it was too close to the morgue for my comfort.

I slowly moved around to the other rooms, checking the family rooms and the office, quietly whispering Anna's name the whole way. Where was she? She had to be here somewhere. Jason had told her to run, and I'd heard her go.

I carefully made my way up the staircase towards the offices. One by one I searched them, checking every nook large enough for a person to hide. I looked in the bathrooms and closets and behind the desks. Anna wasn't anywhere. She didn't respond to any of my calls to her.

I was at a loss. Where could she have gone? I sat in the chair at Conor's desk to think. Before long, I found I was crying again. I was so tired. I was so scared and had no idea what was next. My only hope was that Alice would come rescue me. My thoughts drifted to Dwayne and how I couldn't save him, and then to Tia. And now Jason was in the hands of that monster. God knew what he was doing to him, and Anna was alone, hiding somewhere. I was alone, too. Michael kept showing up, but he wasn't here now. I let my head drop on the desk and cried. I didn't think about how exposed I was. I stopped thinking about finding Anna. I just cried. I didn't sit up until I heard Michael, once again at my side.

"Beth, you need to get moving. He's finished with Jason and is going to look for you and your friend. The sun will be up in an hour and he said he wants to 'clean up this mess by dawn.' I'm afraid he will find you here."

I stood up. "Thanks, Michael — where did you go?"

"I was watching him. I wanted to make sure you weren't in danger. I wanted to be able to warn you when he was coming," he replied.

I got up and followed Michael from the office. We moved slowly down the stairs. "Wait here," he directed when we reached the bottom. "I'll go see where he is now." He disappeared, leaving me alone again, standing at the bottom of the stairs.

I felt too exposed, so I moved into the reception office and sat on the floor behind the desk. A big shiver ran over me, followed by a deep sigh. I waited for Michael.

I opened my eyes to his voice: "Beth, he's in the chapel looking for you and your friend. You need to move now if you want to look for her."

I slowly got up, realizing how stiff the events of the night had made me.

I checked all the rooms at the front of the old house as I made my way to the casket room. Once again, I whispered Anna's name repeatedly as I moved, a little louder this time. When I got to the kitchen, I paused at the door to the garage before turning the handle and going in. The light coming through the windows was getting brighter. Pre-dawn light. The sun would soon be up. Conor would be in a hurry to finish us off.

I slowly approached the door to the morgue, the room where I had seen two of my best friends, dead. I expected to see Jason this time. I silently opened the door and stepped through. I wasn't ready for what waited for me.

Two steps into the morgue and I saw Jason on one of the metal tables. I immediately began to gag and vomited all over the floor. My face and forehead turned clammy, and I broke out in a cold sweat. Once I was sure it was over, I spat on the floor a couple of times and then wiped my mouth with the hem of my shirt. I looked at Jason again.

Conor had performed an autopsy. I didn't dare to go closer yet. Jason's face was so pale. His hands were laid beside his body and, like his head, were posed on top of black blocks to ensure they didn't fall. His chest was cut open. His skin was drawn back, revealing muscle and fat tissue on the flaps. There was a little bit of blood on the floor and some still dripping on the table. Everything looked moist. Conor had cut the front of Jason's rib cage off to reveal the cavity that had once held his organs. The ribs lay on the table between his ankles. I could see inside his body. There was a nasty odour hanging in the air.

I took one step and then another towards Jason's lifeless, mutilated body. I stopped halfway to vomit again. This time there was nothing left to come up but a little clear liquid. It was more like dry heaving. I felt light-headed but kept moving. I reached Jason and noticed a metal pail sitting between his legs. I looked inside to see what looked like organs.

I retched for the third time. My empty stomach twisted painfully.

Jason was completely naked other than a piece of cloth covering his groin. I took his hand and began to cry, again. I'm not sure how I had any tears left.

"Jason," I sobbed. "Oh, Jason. Why is this happening to us? We just wanted to see a ghost. We didn't do anything but break in. We weren't trying to hurt anything. Oh, Jason, I love you."

I collapsed on the floor, pulling his hand down with me. I held it against my cheek. It was so cold.

I don't know how long I had been sitting there, but suddenly Michael was beside me again.

"Beth! Beth!" he hissed. "You have to hide. He's coming! He's almost here. Hide fast!"

Terrified, I jumped up and looked for a place to hide. I took a couple of quick steps towards the garage.

"There isn't time!" Michael almost yelled. "Get in there." He pointed to the wall of doors: the fridge doors, where the bodies were kept.

I ran and selected a drawer. Occupied. I slid it back in and slid out another. Empty. I quickly climbed onto the steel bed and pulled it and myself back into the wall, closing the fridge door behind me just as the door to the front hallway opened.

My fridge door didn't close properly, and I could see into the room. I watched as Conor came through the door backward. He was pulling a stretcher behind him. I gasped, clasping my mouth with my hand. Anna was on the table, and she was still alive!

Conor stepped in the pool of vomit I had left on the floor. He stopped and looked down, trying to figure out what he had just stepped in. Then he turned slowly around, scanning the room. He knew I had been there. A smile appeared on his face as he continued to pull the stretcher towards Jason's table.

CHAPTER 31

Conor stood by Jason's body and considered it for a moment. Then he took the bucket and dumped its contents into a bag, placing the bag inside Jason's chest cavity. Then he took the half of Jason's rib cage and put it on top. Lastly, he folded Jason's skin back into place. His chest and stomach were sunken in, but at least I didn't have to stare at his opened body anymore.

"I'm so sorry, Jason," I mouthed.

Conor wiped the remaining blood from the table and from Jason's body and moved him aside, closer to the crematorium. Then he went to Anna, who was struggling against the restraints of the stretcher. That's when I noticed the gag in her mouth. Her eyes were wide with terror, and I could hear her muffled screams as Conor moved her into position.

Conor brushed Anna's hair from her face. "Well, dear, here we are. My work is almost complete, and the night is almost done. I'll take care of you, and then I'll go find your friend, and all will be accomplished. I must thank you, of course. Without your . . . offering, I never would have had the chance to practice, and I do love to practice. You see, when a client comes to me, I want to ensure I do everything correctly. I don't want to make any more mistakes. Ever since that young boy, I've practiced as much as possible so that I will always be aware of the difference between a live person's bleeding and a dead person's bloodletting."

Anna continued to struggle as he spoke. She tried to scream, over and over. I heard the muffled sounds of her voice. Her head snaped back and forth. Her shoulders and arms strained to get free of the straps that held her to the stretcher. Her knees bent ever so slightly, and her ankles flexed as she attempted to free her legs.

Conor had turned to the steel counter to prepare his tools, and my view was partially blocked by the door in front of me. He turned and I could see that he held a syringe. Anna must have seen it as well, because she started to struggle with more effort and passion. Her screams came with more frequency and volume.

"Now, now, my dear. No need to struggle. You need not fear this needle. You won't feel but a little sting. It's just a little something to calm you down, so that I can release the restraints and get you onto a proper table. We wouldn't want to get blood all over this nice stretcher now, would we?"

He grabbed her head, turning it to the side and I watched as he plunged the syringe into her neck and pushed the clear liquid out of the barrel and into her body. He turned to the sink and disposed of the syringe in a yellow container marked SHARPS. I looked back to Anna, who was still struggling, but seemed to have tired.

Conor looked back over his shoulder at Anna. "How are you feeling my dear? A little more relaxed? I'll be there in just a moment. I'm just getting my tools ready. I need to be properly prepared to perform the embalming."

Anna managed a moan, but she was no longer struggling at her restraints. What could I do? I had to try to save her! I began to move when Michael appeared next to me. "Don't," he said. "I can't keep you safe out there right now. If you go out, he will kill you."

I froze. There was nothing I could do.

Conor moved to Anna's side and placed a tray filled with instruments on a cart next to him. "Now, you might find this a little embarrassing, but please don't worry. I'm a professional and will look after you with care," he said as he picked up her right arm. He bent it at the elbow and pulled her shirt sleeve off. Then he went around and did the same with her left arm. Once he had her arms out, he removed her shirt over her head and placed it in a bag.

Anna only moaned.

Conor reached out and undid her shorts and pulled down the zipper. He rolled her slightly and pulled them down over her left hip, then walked around and repeated the process at her right hip, and then slid off the shorts, placing them in the same bag as her shirt. Anna was now lying on the table almost naked.

"Please don't take off her underwear." I said to myself. The words fell on deaf ears as Conor reached up and gently removed her underwear, covering her groin with a small white cloth.

Next, he propped Anna up, reached around, and undid her bra. He removed it and placed it, along with the underwear, in the bag.

"Now, dear, I need to ensure that your body is clean and sanitized. I promise I will respect you through the whole process. I'll use warm soap and water. Afterall, you've been running around in here for hours. I'm sure you worked up a sweat along the way." Conor filled a small metal bowl with soap and water and took a sponge and began to wash Anna's body. He started with her feet and legs. He was careful to avoid her genitals. I watched as he washed her hips and stomach moving towards her breasts.

"Now I need to clean your breasts," he said. "Don't worry. I'll be gentle, and I take no perverted bliss out of doing it. It's merely procedure."

Once he finished her torso, he washed her armpits and arms. He cleaned her neck and face and then set the bowl on the counter.

"Now I need to spray you with a sanitizer. It's not toxic, but it does smell a little. Allow me to put some cotton in your nose so the smell doesn't bother you." Conor took two cotton sticks and put one in each nostril, and then proceeded to spray Anna from head to toe.

"I'll need to leave that to dry, and then we will get started," he told Anna.

Conor turned his attention to Jason. "Well, sir, we seem to be pretty much finished with you. All we need to do is get you into the fire. One moment and I'll be back."

As he turned towards the garage door, he saw the vomit on the floor again and stopped, considering. He turned and surveyed the room. He looked at Jason. "It seems you've had a visitor, young man. Any chance you can tell me where she went? I would like to make her acquaintance." The monster went to the corner, grabbed a mop, and cleaned up my mess. Then he returned the mop to its place.

Conor opened the door to the garage and disappeared. I was braving myself to get out and help Anna when the door opened again, and Conor wheeled in a wooden casket. It was nothing fancy. It didn't even look to be varnished or stained. He pushed it over next to Jason's body.

"Now let's get you into bed, young sir," he told Jason. "You will be much more comfortable. There's a nice straw mattress beneath the satin sheets."

Conor pulled Jason's feet over into the casket, followed by his hips, torso and head. It took just a minute, and Jason was at rest. I knew what was next. Cremation.

He turned his attention back to Anna. "Well, my sweet, are you ready? Have no fear, you won't feel a thing. That shot I gave you should take care of any pain, and then you'll simply drift off into a deep sleep."

Conor went to a big vat-looking thing by the sink and filled it with water. "Normally I would use embalming chemicals," he told Anna, "but as I'm going to cremate you so soon, I'll just practice with warm water."

He took a hose directly from the sink and ran water along the table. I watched as the water washed up along Anna's body and ran down the small troughs at the sides of the table, then drained through the hole in the table and was piped back to the sink. He turned a valve on the big vat full of water and brought a hose over and hooked it under Anna's arm.

Next, he picked up a scalpel and looked at it. "Now, my dear, this won't be fun for you." Anna didn't move. I prayed that she was unconscious. "I'm going to make a small incision along your shoulder, using your clavicle as a backboard to ensure my cut is true. Once I do that, I'll find your carotid artery and jugular vein and open them up. I'll be slipping the tip of the hose into your artery, and it will slowly push the blood from your body, out the jugular and then down the drain. Any questions?" He paused. "Of course not," he laughed.

Conor picked up the scalpel and made a two-inch cut on Anna's clavicle. There wasn't as much blood as I expected. He used something like a pair of scissors and cut something I couldn't see beneath the skin. It took several small snips. He used a hook tool and fished around in the hole and brought out what looked like a piece of linguini, about the width of a milkshake straw. He passed a piece of string under it and then fished in Anna's clavicle for something else. I didn't see what it was, but he passed the string beneath it as well.

More blood washed down the table.

Conor picked up the scalpel and cut what I assumed was an artery, slicing it halfway through. There was a lot of blood when he did that. It didn't exactly pump as you'd see in a horror movie, but there was a lot of blood, and it was pumping. I gagged, covering my mouth, not wanting to give away my position.

Then he put the end of the hose into the artery, stopping the bleeding momentarily as he made a cut in the vein, which he left open for the blood to run. He turned a knob on the end of the hose, and in a few seconds, water was going in and blood was coming out.

"Please forgive me," Conor spoke gently now, "but I need to massage your limbs to ensure the water moves through them." With that, he picked up Anna's hand and began to rub the fingers and the palm. I watched as he massaged her arms and legs and feet as well. I watched as the blood slowly got thinner and clearer until eventually it was simply water running from the table. My best friend was now pale and lifeless.

Conor turned off the vat and gently removed the hose from Anna's neck. He took a needle and some thread and stitched up the small incision. Then he took a towel and dried her body and the table.

"Now, I'm not one to waste," Conor announced to the room. I'm assuming he was speaking to one or both of the bodies. "I noticed the two of you are quite close, likely boyfriend and girlfriend, am I right? I think so. What I propose is that you share this casket." He pointed to the casket where Jason lay. "What do you think, dear? Sir? No objections? Good, then it's settled." He wheeled the casket over to Anna and shoved her into it so that she and Jason were in an eternal embrace.

"Sorry for the bumpy move, dear. I just assumed you would be more comfortable in your lover's arms for eternity than you would simply laying on top of him."

He picked up a piece of wood and his drill, and screwed a lid on over their legs and lower torsos. Then he screwed on a second piece over their heads. He lay the drill on a table and rolled the casket towards the crematorium door, whistling that awful song.

CHAPTER 32

I WAITED THIRTY SECONDS and then whispered, "Michael, can you see if he's coming back?"

Michael disappeared and then came back a few seconds later. "He's busy getting them into the crematorium," he reported. "I think you've got a couple of minutes."

I nodded and pushed the door to my hiding place open, being careful not to make any noise. As I balanced on the edge, stretching my feet towards the floor, the bed slid open. I hung on tight until the ride was over. There was a slight squeak and a thud as the bed reached full extension. I dropped to the ground as quietly as I could and stopped dead, listening.

When I didn't hear anything, I made for the door. I didn't waste time trying to hide the fact that I'd been there. I simply left my drawer open, snuck out the front door, turned left and headed for the chapel.

The day was getting brighter. It was five o'clock. People would soon start moving about the town. If I could get back up in the bell tower, maybe one of those windows would open, or at least break. Maybe then I could signal or call out to someone. I wasn't that far from the town square. Didn't Bel say she took fresh produce and eggs to the market around this time?

Although I knew where Conor was, I was still as quiet as I could be. No sense in letting him know what direction I had gone. If he was going to get me too, I might as well make him work for it. I had no idea how long it would take for him to get Jason and Anna into the crematorium. It could be mere minutes before he came looking for me. I knew he was going to be in a hurry. Could I use that to my advantage?

I would need to defend myself. As I passed by a storage closet, I opened it and looked in. The only weapon I could see was a broom handle. I took it and screwed its head off as I entered the chapel. A sudden warmth came over me as I entered. It was comforting, like the feeling you get when you come home after being away for a while. The sanctuary must have been warming up as the sun glimmered through the stained glass.

I made my way around the perimeter hallway to the front entry. The only helpful thing I could see was the chair I had used to climb on Jason's shoulders. I saw the blood stain on the floor where Conor had beat him, providing Anna with her escape. Maybe I could pull myself up using the chair again.

Setting my makeshift staff against the wall, I put the chair under the trap door and jumped. I caught the lip on my third try, but there was no way I could pull myself up and in. I knocked the chair over several times, trying to use it for leverage to give myself a boost. But I was not getting up there without help.

I stepped down off the chair and looked around. Nothing. I tried the door again out of shear desperation, but it was firmly locked. Frustrated, I threw the chair at a window, but like the others, these windows were made to withstand force. I was out of options.

I ran for the back door. Maybe it would open?

As I was running down the centre aisle, the broom handle got caught on a pew. It tripped me and I went flying. I managed to catch my fall but hurt my wrist on the way down. I cried out in pain, rolled over onto my back and sat up. My wrist was swelling up already and it hurt like crazy. I tried making a fist but couldn't. Sharp pains were running up my arm with each attempted move. Moaning, I pulled myself up. I picked up the broom handle and leaned it on the pew.

I took another look at my wrist and realized it was broken. At least it was the left one. I popped open a button on my shirt and tucked my bad wrist into the opening. A makeshift sling. The weight of my arm putting pressure on my wrist caused a stabbing pain that almost made me scream.

I made my way to the back door, more carefully this time. It was locked as I expected, adding to the weight of despair on my heart. I went back out to the sanctuary and sat a few rows back. I didn't know what else to do, so I slid to my knees. If there was ever a time to try prayer, it was now.

"God," I prayed, "it's been a long time since we spoke. I haven't prayed since I thought I was pregnant. I was so angry at everyone when Jason left me. I thought I lost everything. And now, my friends are dead, and I'm being hunted by a monster. I don't know what to do. I don't know where to hide and I can't get out. If ever I needed you, it's now. Help me," I pleaded. "Please, help me. I don't want to die."

"Well, well, well," Conor interrupted. He was standing just inside the door. I had no idea how long he had been there. "What have I found here? Another little church mouse? What, may I ask, are you doing? Praying? You can't tell me that you believe in all that mumbo-jumbo Jesus stuff, do you?" He took a step into the aisle and held his arms up wide. "Take a look around you. Where are all your friends? Oh, that's right, I killed them. Where was your God when I took their lives? Did you pray for them?" He took a few more steps towards me. "He didn't protect them; do you think he will protect you?" I looked around for something I could do, somewhere I could go — anything — but I was trapped.

"You psycho!" I hissed. "You won't get away with this."

"But I already have," Conor laughed. "Don't you see? This is my house. Everything that happens here is controlled by me. I control who comes in and who goes out. I control who lives and who dies. Your friends are all gone. Not a trace. A sixteen hundred-degree furnace took care of that. No DNA, no dental records, nothing, and now it's your turn. You might as well just give up. Put down the stick and I promise not to make it hurt."

"Not a chance, you monster!" I snarled. "Come near me, and I'll kill you!" I squared my shoulders and struck an awkward, one-handed stance with the broom handle. I must have jostled my wrist because it screamed in pain. I winced. He just laughed at me.

I knew I couldn't escape. I knew I couldn't win in a fight, not with one hand. I had nowhere to turn. I'm going to die, I thought. Tears began to stream down my cheeks.

"Pray." It was a simple word. "Pray." I looked beside me to see Michael standing there. He smiled at me and nodded. "It's ok. I'll keep you safe. Pray."

I slowly sat down on the pew next to me and closed my eyes.

"What are you doing?" yelled Conor. "And you! Why are you interfering? What are you doing here? This is *my house!*"

I began to pray.

"No Conor, this is His house," came the soft reply from Michael, "and He asked me to come take care of it for Him. I think you should go now."

"I'm not going anywhere!" raged Conor.

I kept my eyes shut and continued to pray for God to save me. I said The Lord's Prayer. I remembered it from Sunday School. "Our Father, who art in heaven. Hallowed be thy name."

"This time I'm going to beat you!" Conor screamed.

I heard Conor begin to move.

"Deliver me from evil." Now *that* seemed appropriate.

I heard a fight break out. There was grunting and the clashing of metal. It sounded like a sword fight was taking place above my head. Still, I kept my eyes closed and prayed. Then I heard, "Run now!" and opened my eyes.

I stared, stunned by what I saw.

Michael was standing in the aisle of the sanctuary. He was no longer a little boy. Instead, he stood over six feet tall. He had wings spreading out from his upper back and he was holding a sword above his head. He was glowing. In front of him stood Conor. His eyes burned fiery red. He had a sword too, and it was braced against Michael's, mid-battle in the space between them. I couldn't understand what I was seeing. I knew who they were, but now they were different.

"Run!" Michael ordered. "I've opened the front door, but you need to go — *now*."

I took one unsure step out from my seat, and then another. I turned to move up the aisle just as the fight began again. I glanced back once and saw the swords clashing, and then I just ran. I got to the front door and pushed. It opened with ease.

I stumbled out into the early dawn light.

CHAPTER 33

FROM THE SIDEWALK I turned to watch the funeral home. It wasn't nearly far enough away, but the exhaustion of the last few hours hit me hit me hard. I had no choice but to stop or fall over. Usually, fresh air revitalizes me, but this time it worked in reverse.

I took stock of myself. I was alive. I had a broken wrist. I had a many cuts and bruises, but nothing life-threatening. I smelled of sweat. I looked horrible. I *felt* horrible. I had someone's blood on my shirt. Maybe mine?

I half-walked, half-jogged to the town square, where the sheriff's office was. The pain from my wrist was practically blinding me, and I almost ran into Bel as she was heading back to her car after dropping her produce at the market.

"Bel!" I cried. "Oh, thank God it's you." I collapsed at her feet sobbing. Everything — all the emotions, the fear, the sorrow, the pain, everything was coming out all at once.

"Beth?" she gasped. "What's wrong? What happened? Are you okay?"

She knelt beside me and pulled the hair out of my eyes. I saw her expression change from inquisitive to intense concern. Her eyes moved from my face to my arm, still tucked inside my shirt.

"We need to get you some help," she decided. "Who did this to you? I'm calling 911."

"No, wait," I told her. "Call this number." I pulled Alice's card from my pocket. I was happy that I'd kept it after I called.

Bel dialed the number on the card. "Hello, is this Trooper Alice Maxwell? My name is Bel, and I'm here with Beth Springle. Yes, she's okay. Well sort of. She looks terrible, and I think she has a broken arm. No, she's alone. We're in the town square. I'm not sure what happened, she hasn't told me yet. No, we haven't called 911 yet. Beth asked me to call you first. Okay, I'll hang up and call 911. Yes, we will wait for you here. Thanks."

I looked up at Bel who had stood to make the call, "Thank you," I almost whispered.

Bel dialed again. "Hello, 911? This is Isobel Ramirez. I'm in the town square in Harrington, Maine. My friend needs an ambulance. I think she was attacked. It looks like she has a broken arm, and she has lots of other bruises and cuts . . . Yes, she's conscious. She looks awful . . . Just a minute . . . Beth, can I check your pulse?" I held out my good wrist. "It's about 90 beats per minute," she said into the phone. "No, it was steady, and I found it first try. A blanket? I think I can find something. Okay, we'll wait here in the square. How long will it be? Okay thanks." Bel hung up the phone.

Bel bent down and helped me get up. We walked over to a bench by the fountain. I made sure I could see in the direction of the funeral home. "I'm going to go get you a blanket and some water," she told me.

"No, please don't leave me," I begged her. "I can't stay here alone. He might come after me."

"Who?" she asked.

"Conor. Conor O'Reagan, the funeral guy. He killed my friends and now he's after me." I told her.

Bel's face took on a look of shock and fear. "What? Are you sure it was Conor? He killed your friends? Where is he?" She looked around warily.

"Inside the funeral home. He killed them all! He burned their bodies. Michael got me out. He saved me." I was sobbing once more — blubbering, more like it.

Bel held me as we waited for Alice and the ambulance. She didn't say a word. She simply held me in her arms and rocked gently.

A few minutes later, we heard a siren coming our way. It was too soon to be the ambulance; they were at least thirty minutes out. Thirty seconds later, Sheriff Johnson pulled up to a screeching halt. He jumped out of the car ran towards us.

"What the hell is going on?" he barked, as he looked me up and down. His tone softened, slightly. "What happened to you, young lady? You're a mess. Are you hurt?"

"Mostly my wrist," I replied. "I think the rest of me is okay."

"What happened? Did you fall or something? It's awfully early for you concert folks to be up wandering about." His tone wasn't what I would expect from someone who was supposed to be there to help me.

"Yes," I responded. "I fell when I was running and hurt my wrist. I think it's broken. Bel called 911 for me, and an ambulance is coming." I didn't say anything about the funeral home. I had an uneasy feeling, remembering how Conor spoke about the sheriff, like they were old friends. "How did you know I was here?" I asked him.

"I was called by a concerned citizen," he said. "They told me that they saw a young woman running around screaming about a ghost or something. Have you had any alcohol or taken any drugs?" He asked. "I know you and your friends are from Canada. You do know that marijuana isn't legal here, right?"

"No, I haven't had anything to drink, and I don't do drugs," I responded. I must have rolled my eyes or given him a look.

"Don't you give me attitude, young lady," he scolded. "I can just as soon put you in a jail cell while you wait for the ambulance. I have it on good authority that some young people broke into the funeral home tonight and vandalized it. Was that you and your friends?"

How did he know about the funeral home? Had Conor called him to clean up his mess? Was the sheriff in on it?

"I'm tired," was all I said. I closed my eyes and leaned my head on Bel's shoulder.

"You didn't answer my question, young lady," he pressed. "Did you or did you not break into the funeral home tonight?"

I didn't respond. I didn't even open my eyes. I was just too tired, and I was sure nothing more could happen to me with Bel beside me. I felt as safe as I could under the circumstances.

"If you don't answer, you'll give me no choice," the sheriff went on. "You are under arrest for suspicion of break and enter and vandalism. Stand up. I'm taking you to our lock-up.

The ambulance can treat you there when they come, but you aren't going anywhere until you tell me the truth."

He grabbed me under the good arm and tried to lift me up. I didn't help. I was too tired. Instead, I sat there like a rag doll. Bel stood up and got in his way.

"Sheriff," she said, "don't you think she's been through enough, without you manhandling her? She's got a broken arm and looks like she's been through hell and back. Perhaps you could get her a bottle of water and a blanket? We can sort all this out once she's been checked over and had her injuries looked after."

A big huff was the only response I heard, and then he stormed off. I smiled.

"That won't keep him away for long, but I think you'll get that water and blanket." Bel smiled too.

"How did he hear about me?" I asked Bel. "Would 911 call him? Wouldn't they just send an ambulance for a broken arm?"

"I'm not sure," she shrugged, "Maybe a concerned citizen did call. Or maybe 911 called so he could be here to assist before the ambulance got here. Either way, his attitude stinks." I broke down again. A river of tears flowed down my cheeks as Bel held me.

The sheriff returned with a blanket and bottle of water. Once I had taken a drink, he stood tall: "Elizabeth Springle, you are hereby under arrest for the crimes of breaking and entering, vandalism, and theft." He took my good arm and cuffed it to the bench. I was too tired to protest.

Just as he finished, a state police car roared into a parking space across the street.

CHAPTER 34

ALMOST BEFORE THE car stopped, Trooper Alice Maxwell was out and marching over to us. "Alice Maxwell," she said as she put her hand out to Sheriff Johnson. "Who is Beth Springle?"

"I . . . I am," I managed. "Thank you for coming."

"Why the hell is she handcuffed to a park bench?" Alice demanded. "Why is a victim being treated this way?"

"Victim? She's my perpetrator. I've charged her with breaking and entering, vandalism, and theft. She practically confessed to the B and E. I placed her in custody," retorted the sheriff.

I had to give some props to Alice, the way she took charge.

"Victim. She's been terrorized by a maniac in the funeral home. Why do you think I'm here, officer? Uncuff this *victim,* immediately. Have you even had her arm looked at? Gotten her something to eat?" Alice took out her own keys and undid my restraints. Just then four more state trooper cars arrived, and a dozen officers got out.

Alice turned her attention to the group. "The perpetrator is in the funeral home. His name is Conor O'Reagan. Ensure that all the exits are covered and then move in. Secure the offender and bring him over to the sheriff's office. Officer Johnson here has offered to let us use his station as our headquarters. Isn't that right sir?" She gave a hard look at the sheriff who simply nodded.

"It's Sheriff Johnson," he mumbled.

I watched as the officers dispersed and surrounded the funeral home complex. "The windows don't break," I told her, "And the doors have some kind of hidden lock on them so they don't open."

Alice spoke into a microphone "The windows may be bullet proof and the doors apparently have some sort of hidden locking mechanism. Do whatever it takes to get in. The suspect is likely destroying evidence."

As she finished, the ambulance finally arrived. One paramedic took my pulse and blood pressure on my good arm while the other looked at my wrist. I winced as she touched it. She applied slight pressure all around. "I think it's broken and possibly dislocated as well," she said. "You need to get to the ER for X-rays and have a doctor take a look."

"Can it wait for a little?" Alice asked. "I need to ask her some questions."

"We can't wait," was the response. "We need to be closer to Millinocket if we're not on a call. You could take her to the hospital on your way back, maybe?"

Trooper Alice thought for a minute and nodded. "I think that would be okay. Is that alright with you?" she asked me.

I nodded. "Any chance I can get something for the pain?"

The EMT went to the ambulance and came back with a small paper cup. Inside were two pills. "Tylenol," she told me. "Sorry, it's all I can offer."

I popped both pills into my mouth and washed them down with a drink of water.

"It's settled then," Alice confirmed. "Can you splint her up and do anything else she may need before you go? Let me know if I need to watch for anything?"

"Absolutely," was the response.

Once my arm had been splinted, they gave Alice some instructions I didn't hear, and they left.

"Sheriff, I need you to come with me as we gain entry. Mr. O'Reagan may be more compliant if he hears a voice he knows." The sheriff reluctantly went with her.

"How are you feeling?" Bel asked me as we watched the action across the street. It was the first time she'd spoken in a while.

"Better, actually," I said. "The Tylenol is starting to work. The water helped too. I haven't eaten anything since the concert, so I'm hungry. Mostly, I'm just really tired."

Police cars lined the yard of the funeral home, and about a dozen officers had surrounded the building. I could see officers at the front doors to the funeral home and the church trying to get them open. They weren't having any success. A couple of other officers were trying to break windows, but no one was making any progress.

Then I watched as Alice got in one of the police cars. She backed it up to the edge of the parking lot and then shot it straight at the main entrance of the funeral home. Her passenger's side front bumper bashed the door, the door frame, and part of the wall right into the lobby of the funeral home. The car reversed and parked back in the lot.

"What are you waiting for?" Alice hollered. "Get in there before he destroys any more evidence!"

Five or six of the officers went inside while the rest maintained the perimeter in case Conor made a break for it.

As we waited, Sheriff Johnson wandered back over to where we stood. He didn't say a word.

The parking lot was brightly lit by the morning sun when two officers finally led a handcuffed Conor through the rubble of the front door and into a waiting police car.

As they headed down the road to Millinocket, Alice walked back across the street and stopped beside us. Sheriff Johnson had simply stood by and watched the events unfold.

"We are taking him to town for questioning," she told the sheriff. "I've got a team guarding the alleged crime scene until the Evidence Response Team arrives. We would appreciate it if you and your team would secure Mr. O'Reagan's residence. I understand it's one of the homes across the street. We would ask that no one, not even one of your officers, enters the residence, so we can preserve any evidence that might be inside. I'm going to transport Beth to the hospital. You're welcome to follow us if you've got questions for her. From what I've seen inside, the 'alleged' part is looking more and more like it will be dropped. Bel, do you want to come with us?"

Bel looked at me as I nodded to her. "Yes." she said.

Then Officer Alice turned to me. "Okay Beth, are you ready to go? You'll be in the back seat, if that's okay, and Bel can ride with you. On the way, I'll have the camera running so we can talk, is that okay? While you aren't a suspect at this time, you are still entitled to remain silent and to have us contact a lawyer on your behalf."

"That would be fine," I replied. "Ask me anything you want. I don't need a lawyer. Can someone please call my parents?"

"I already did, dear. I let them know that there was an incident, but that you were fine other than an injured wrist. They'll be met at the border by one of our officers and escorted directly to the hospital," she said. "By the time we get there ourselves, get you registered and looked at, they should be there. Now, let's the three of us get in the car and go. Shall we?"

Alice led the way to her police car and opened the door for me, closing it gently after she helped me with my seatbelt. As we backed out of the parking spot, I looked at Sheriff Johnson. He was still just standing there. He glared back at me, shook his head, and then turned away.

Bel held my hand for the entire forty-minute drive to the hospital. Trooper Maxwell waited until we were clear of town before she asked, "Can you tell me what happened last night? Please remember that you don't need to say anything, and that the camera will be running."

I took a minute and gathered my thoughts. "It all started when the guys wanted to see that ghost we heard about. Last night, or I guess the night before, we sat around the town square for most of the night hoping to see it, but then Sheriff Johnson ran us off. That's when the guys hatched the plan to sneak into the funeral home to watch for the ghost there. I didn't want to, but everyone else was in, so I went along. After the concert, we got off the bus at the town square, and Dwayne used a lock pick thing to get us in at the back of the church."

I told her every detail I could think of. Alice didn't interrupt except to ask for clarification, like when I first told her about Michael helping us. And she wanted to know who attacked who when Conor smashed Dwayne against the wall.

I described what Conor had done to Dwayne while I watched through the camera; how I was helpless to save him from the crematorium. All Conor's threats, and his hints that we weren't the first to fall at his hands.

I remembered to tell her about my climbing up into the bell tower to call her because our cell phones didn't work in the funeral home, and that all of our phones had died.

My words caught as I tried to give her details about how I'd found Jason. I was able to talk about puking, but beyond that, I just couldn't. I stopped talking for a few minutes as Bel leaned over and hugged me.

I continued with the details about hiding and watching as he killed Anna. I felt so ashamed that I hadn't tried to help. Alice told me there was nothing I could have done, and that I would have ended up dead myself. Then no one would know what had happened.

I finished with the impossible. I left out the details about Michael's transformation. I said only that, somehow, he had come between me and Conor and had told me to run, and that the door had somehow been unlocked.

Neither Alice nor Bel challenged anything I said. Bel simply smiled and squeezed my hand.

CHAPTER 35

WE PULLED INTO Millinocket Regional Hospital. The emergency and main entrances were one and the same. The building had lots of glass along the top. Inside were rows of pink and white chairs.

"You two take a seat, and I'll get you registered," said Alice. I watched as she headed off towards the registration desk.

She returned a few minutes later with a nurse who led us down a linoleum tile hallway and into a treatment room. I was told a doctor would be with me as soon as possible. I lay on a bed and closed my eyes, but only for a minute. Every time I closed my eyes, I saw Conor standing in front of Michael, their swords clashing. I could see Conor's eyes glowing red, and I'm not sure if it was a memory or a projection, but his mouth and nostrils breathed fire. I wanted my mom and dad to hurry and get here.

Another nurse came in and brought me a gown. She asked if I could take off my shirt and slip into it. When I nodded, she assisted me in getting it off, taking great care to protect my injured left wrist.

As the shirt came off, I realized just how filthy I was and how much blood was on me — blood and vomit. I realized how much I smelled, too. Tears ran down my cheeks as another wave of sorrow washed over me. The nurse acted like she didn't notice and helped me wash myself. As we finished getting my gown on, the doctor walked in.

"Beth Springle?" she asked. "I understand you've had a rough night. Do you mind if I examine you?" I nodded my consent. "My name is Doctor Nancy Jones, but you can call me Nancy if you wish. Now, let's start with your arm." She reached out and gently took my arm in hers and tenderly removed the splint. I couldn't squeeze her finger very hard when she asked, and I cried out in pain when she tried to turn it, even slightly, while she held my hand.

She checked my vision, looked in my ears and examined each and every bruise and scrape on my body, from head to toe. "Is there any reason I might need to do a rape kit?" she asked me.

"No, no one touched me like that," I said.

"Okay, let's get you to X-ray for that wrist. Nurse, can you page Ortho? I'd like them to take a look at the X-rays when they come in. Also, let's hang a bag of saline and give her five milligrams of morphine to help with the pain. It's going to hurt when they X-ray it.

"Alright Beth, I'll be back once you return from X-ray, and we'll go from there. The good news is that other than your wrist, you appear not to have sustained any other major injuries. Has your family been called?"

I nodded my response as my new trooper friend answered, "Yes, her parents are on the way down from New Brunswick. They should be here in about an hour."

"Terrific. We should know more about that wrist by the time they arrive. I'll see you soon, Beth." The doctor left the room, pausing to sanitize her hands at the doorway. The nurse went about hanging an IV for me, inserting the needle into the back of my good hand.

I turned to Bel, "Thanks for coming with me, Bel. I'm sorry to ruin your day. Will your dad be worried?"

"I wouldn't leave if you wanted me to," she said. "And don't worry about my dad. Trooper Alice called him and explained the situation. Everyone in town knows what's going on by now."

Eventually, an orderly came in and I got in the wheelchair he was pushing. He hung the IV on the chair and pushed me down the hall to X-ray. I looked back at Belle and Alice as I was wheeled away.

"We'll be right here when you get back," Bel called as we went around a corner and they disappeared.

The doctor was right when she told me it would hurt while they took the X-rays. The technician apologized every time she needed to take a different view. I hissed and moaned in agony as she got me lay my wrist down in different positions. I didn't need to move it exactly, but the pain of picking it up and putting it down again while twisting from the shoulder and elbow to accommodate each new position sent pain screaming up my arm. I wondered if the nurse had forgotten the morphine.

After what seemed like an eternity, the technician helped me back into the wheelchair and rolled me back to my room.

I arrived to find Bel waiting alone. She was eating a small can of plain pringles and a drinking a Coke.

"Coke for breakfast?" I joked.

"Breakfast? This is lunch. It's almost noon." she said.

I couldn't believe it was almost noon. The thought of the time woke up my stomach and it began to grumble. A nurse's aide helped me back into my bed and gave me a blanket, which I gladly accepted. I was cold and this thin hospital gown wasn't very warm.

I had been lying there only a few minutes when Trooper Maxwell came back.

"I found a couple of people who are anxious to see you." she smiled.

My parents walked in. Mom pushed past everyone and ran to my side. She wrapped me in her arms and whispered, "I love you." Luckily, she was on my right side and missed my wounded wing. "Oh, my baby!" she kept saying. Tears were in her eyes, and I was crying again. I don't know how I had any tears left to cry.

I looked over and saw my dad just standing there, about five feet away. He, too, was crying. I held out my arm and he came over, bent down, and hugged me. Then Mom joined back in, and we had a group hug.

"I see Mom and Dad have arrived." Doctor Nancy had returned.

"Hi, doc," I greeted her. "Yes, these are my folks, Ben and Emily. So, what's the word from X-ray?"

"It's like I thought. You have a displaced fracture called a Colles fracture. What that means is that the radius, the bone on your thumb side, is broken near the end by the wrist and the broken part is tilted up. I've spoken with Orthopedics, and they recommend surgery as soon as possible to repair it. With your consent, I'll let the team know. They think they can fit your surgery in this afternoon as they've had a cancellation."

I started crying again, and Mom ran her finger through my hair and stroked my face. "Shh," she whispered. "Mommy's here now. Everything will be OK. Now, who is this beautiful young woman?"

"Hi, Mrs. Springle. I'm Bel," she replied, stretching out her hand.

Mom stood up and gave her a hug. "Are you the one that's been watching out for my baby? Thank you for looking after her."

The rest of that afternoon is very fuzzy. Between answering questions, pleading for food (but not being allowed any), and then going under for the surgery, time became a blur. All I remembered later was waking up in a hospital room, surrounded by my folks, Bel, and Alice. My throat was so dry it felt like I was swallowing knives. I tried to speak but couldn't get the words out.

Mom reached over and put a straw in my mouth. "Here, honey, take a sip." I've never enjoyed a sip of water more than I did that evening.

"Bel," I managed, "you're still here. Don't you have to get back home? Your parents will be worried sick."

"It's okay. I wanted to be here when you woke up. My dad is on his way to get me." Then she confused me. "I'm sorry," she said as she hung her head. "It's all my fault."

"What do you mean?" I asked her. "You didn't do anything. You weren't even there."

"If I hadn't told you about the ghost, you wouldn't have tried to see it. I'm so sorry." She shook her head and started to cry.

I reached out and took her hand, pulling her closer. I wrapped my one good arm around her neck "You have nothing to be sorry for, Bel. You just told us a story. Nothing more. You didn't break into a funeral home. You didn't kill my friends. You didn't try to kill me. All of that was us and Conor. You had nothing to do with it." I tried to console her, but I knew she still blamed herself.

"I actually need to thank you, Bel. You called Alice again. You stayed with me. You've been a good friend."

A nurse, whose name tag said "Angela," walked into the room. "How is my patient? Awake, I see," she made a note on my chart. "So how are you feeling, Beth? How's the pain?"

"I'm good. Just a little pain. I'm hungry, though." I told her.

"I'll see what I can find for you to eat," she told me. "As for the rest of you, I need to ask you to leave. Our little lamb needs time to rest. Visiting hours begin at nine a.m. Feel free to come back then."

My parents said good night and promised to be back in the morning. Bel gave me a hug and promised to call. Alice left me another of her cards in case I needed her or remembered anything else.

Ten minutes later, Angela came back with an applesauce muffin, a vanilla pudding, and two pieces of toast with some peanut butter on the side. "Sorry," she apologized. "The cafeteria is closed, and it's the best I could do. I promise you'll have a big breakfast waiting for you." She had a nice smile and a very comforting way about her.

I ate the toast and peanut butter along with the pudding but saved the muffin in case I got hungry later overnight.

Alone in the silent room, I realized just how tired I really was. I wasn't sure how much I could sleep, though. Each time I closed my eyes, the events of the previous night started replaying in my head. Then I suddenly remembered: my phone. I'd left it up in the bell tower. I needed to call Alice and let her know.

I buzzed the nurse and told her that I needed to make a call. She moved my room's phone to within my reach, and I dialed. Alice answered on the first ring.

"Hi, it's Beth. I just remembered something. I left my cell phone up in the bell tower. It died while I was calling you and then when Jason and Conor started fighting below, I set it down and forgot it. It has some videos on it — probably shakier than the ones from the cameras, but there could be something useful."

"What cameras?"

"The video cameras. The whole funeral home has cameras all over. I was able to watch on the computer in Conor's office. They cover almost every inch of the place. It's how I knew where he was, until he turned them off."

"That's great!" Alice exclaimed. "I'll call the team and let them know. Maybe we can recover some video of what actually happened last night. Video evidence to corroborate your story will go a long way towards putting Conor behind bars and keeping you out. We still need to talk about you breaking into the funeral home. Not to worry, though. I know you've been through the ringer, and I'm on your side, so you just get some sleep, let the investigative team do their job, and we'll get the truth out. Good night, Beth."

"Good night." I handed the phone back to the nurse.

"I heard you had a rough twenty-four hours," Angela commented. "The doctor left a standing order for a sleeping aid if you need it. Shall I bring it for you?"

"That might be a good idea," I admitted. "Every time I close my eyes, all I can see is last night. I think I'll need it if I'm to get any sleep tonight."

Angela returned a few minutes later and left after she watched me take the pill. She dimmed the lights on the way out, but not low enough to plunge me into darkness. I think she could tell a little light would be a good thing for me tonight.

CHAPTER 36

I WOKE UP THE next morning to the sound of singing. Angela was just bringing in my breakfast. "Good morning, Beth," she sang. "You had a good sleep last night. I came to check on you about an hour after you took the pill, and you were out. You slept a good ten hours, but now it's time to get up. I promised you a big breakfast, and I dare say I delivered. It helps to have a friend in the kitchen." She smiled as she opened up the food tray. Inside she revealed something out of a Denny's picture book. There were two pancakes, sausages, bacon, two eggs, and some oatmeal. There was even some maple syrup that said, "Made in Canada." I dug in ravenously.

"Whoa, slow down, dear," she cautioned, "You've barely eaten in the last twenty-four hours. Go slow or you'll be giving it back quicker than it went down."

I laughed so hard I almost choked on my food. "I'm just so hungry!" I told her. "It's delicious. Give my compliments to your chef friend, and thank you for the hookup."

Just then my folks came in. My mom's face lit up when she saw me.

"Good morning, sweetheart," said my mom. Dad followed her in. When he saw me up and eating, he slid past her and sat on the edge of my bed. He took my hand.

"I was so worried about you, Pea," he said. Dad had been calling me "Pea" since I was a little kid. It started out as "Sweet Pea," but got shortened by the time I reached middle school.

"You gave us a quite a scare. When Officer Alice called, she didn't give us any details, only that there'd been an incident, that you were okay, and that we should meet you here at the hospital. She even arranged for a police escort from the border." Dad continued. "How are you feeling?"

"I'm okay," I told them. "Just really tired." I paused for an awkward moment. "I'm sorry," I muttered.

"Oh, honey, you don't need to be sorry." The three of us cried as we embraced each other.

A knock at the door interrupted us. "Pardon the interruption to the family reunion." It was Alice. "I just wanted to check in and see how our girl was doing, and give you an update on where we stand. First, Beth, I've been speaking with the ADA, and if the evidence continues to point in the direction that is, there will be no formal charges against you for the breaking and entering at the funeral home. He doesn't feel right prosecuting you after the events that took place, nor does he think he could convince a jury to find you guilty. Even if he did, and he might, given your confession, no judge would sentence you to more than community service."

I sighed with relief. My mom patted my leg and gave me a smile.

"I also wanted to let you know that the forensic team found a mountain of evidence that corroborates most of your story. We found your phone in that bell tower, and we were able to charge it and get the videos you shot. I'm not sure how you thought to take them, given your situation, but they will be very helpful in court. We have now video evidence that shows Mr. O'Reagan attacking Dwayne and Tia and also parts of the fight between him and Jason. And we found the cell phone jammer and the magnetic door locks, just as you said we would.

"We also searched his home and found the hard drive backup for all the cameras. It turns out that he recorded *everything*, so we have more than just your videos to corroborate your story." She paused as if trying to find the right words. "We discovered that you and your friends were not his first victims. He has done this before. We found the IDs he'd kept as trophies from at least a dozen others, going back years, and we believe we will find more before we're done looking."

"Now for more good news. As long as you guarantee you'll return to the US for the trial, the ADA has agreed to allow you to go home once the doctor clears you. She won't press charges for the B and E. We will need you to return as a witness in the trial against Mr. O'Reagan. It will mean meeting with the prosecutor to go over your testimony to prepare for court. It also means that his lawyer will be able to cross examine you, but we will help prepare you for that too. I want you to know how brave I think you are. You went through hell at the hands of that man. But you survived, and that is truly impressive. Bel packed up all of your belongings and those of your friends, and I've brought them with me. Mr. and Mrs. Springle, you have a fine daughter here."

"Thanks," my dad managed. He was crying and smiling at the same time.

Just then we heard a commotion in the hallway. There were several angry voices coming from the hall, and then Jason's father burst through the door to my room. He was being chased by a nurse. "Sir, you can't go in there! Sir!"

I looked at Mom and Dad, not knowing what to do or say.

Alice jumped up and got in front of Jason's father, David, and restrained him as he rushed at me.

"What in the hell did you do to my son? I hold you responsible. He would never break into a funeral home without someone putting crazy ideas in his head. First you claim he got you pregnant and now this?!"

"Excuse me, sir," Alice said as she held him back. "I'm going to have to ask you to leave. This young woman is not only injured and in need of rest, she is a hero. She escaped from a madman, and was able to assist us in the capture and arrest of a serial killer. Now, I am deeply sorry for the loss of your son. But you need to leave. Now." The force in her voice stopped David in his tracks. The nurse grabbed his arm and escorted him out.

"I'll leave you to it, then," said Alice. "Mr. Springle, I will leave the camping gear and things with security. Just ask on the way out and they'll help you with it. And Beth, I'll be in touch several times over the next few weeks to update you on the case and let you know about any legal responsibilities you may have." She left the room.

There was a lot of hugging and crying during the next half hour or so. My parents were in shock, but happy I survived. They didn't blame me for anything, but they did ask me again and again what we were thinking, and how we could have been so stupid. Their visit was cut short to allow me time to rest. I was worried my friends' parents would blame me. When I talked to my parents about it, they assured me that they would come around.

Later that day, the doctor declared me ready to leave. She promised to send copies of my file and X-rays to my doctor, Lee Stickles, back in Fredericton so she could follow up with me in a few days. She encouraged me to continue to drink lots of fluids, eat healthy meals, and get a lot of rest.

By four o'clock on Sunday afternoon, we were in the car and driving home. Jason's parents had come with Anna's, and they were driving Jason's truck home. Tia's folks were in the convoy as well, with Dwayne's folks in the back seat. Four New Brunswick cars made their way up I-95 to the border crossing in Houlton. Trooper Alice Maxwell escorted us all the way to the border where she got out of the car and spoke to Canadian Border Services.

We pulled into our driveway around eight and I went right to bed. Dad came in a few minutes later and sat in the rocking chair. "Mind if I just sit here for a bit?" he asked.

I smiled at him, "I would like that. It makes me feel good knowing you're here."

CHAPTER 37

I SPENT THE NEXT few weeks healing. Mind, body, and spirit.

I had a follow up with my doctor and more X-rays. My wrist was healing nicely, and I would make a full recovery.

Mom and Dad were great. They were there for me but didn't push. They let me talk when I needed to, but they never asked too many questions. I was seeing a psychologist twice a week, talking through my recurring nightmares and working through the stress and fear that remained in my head. I was diagnosed with PTSD and would start with a support group in the following weeks.

My parents believed in Michael when I told them. Alice had suggested that I might want to leave Michael out of my story, but I couldn't keep that part from my parents, nor they from their church friends. Mom's prayer group had gathered at my home and prayed over me on a couple of occasions, and they convinced me to go to church, where the whole congregation clapped for me, and the pastor prayed over me. The church ladies said that God would protect those that believed in Him and had become Christians: He had a whole army of Angels ready to act when necessary. They believed that Michael, God's top archangel, had only appeared when I needed him because I had become a Christian years before, and that even though I didn't go to church anymore, God had vowed to protect his children. They pointed out the symbolism of the church, Michael's connection to me, and the demonic attributes of Conor during the battle.

All I knew was that this little boy had become my saviour. I was grateful for his protection. But I wasn't so sure God would send his best angel to fight my battle.

A large funeral was held at the Aitken University Centre for Jason, Anna, Tia, and Dwayne. Their parents all decided a joint funeral would be the best way to honour my friends. They'd had the chance to work through what had happened and had all come to visit me. I was assured they didn't blame me. I was even seated with the families at the funeral. An urn and a picture of each of them were placed on a table at the front, and dozens of flower arrangements filled the stage. Trooper Alice and Bel sent wreaths. The arena was almost full. Even the mayor and several members of the legislative assembly showed up, and the premier sent a letter to each family, including mine.

Many in attendance made donations to the Canadian Mental Health Association at the request of the families. I heard that over ten thousand dollars was raised over the next few weeks. At least something positive had come out of the nightmare.

About four weeks after I had returned home, a knock came at the door. I was surprised to see Trooper Alice with another woman in an FBI jacket. After giving Alice a big hug, I invited them in, and Mom put on a pot of coffee before she and Dad joined us.

"This is Special Agent Karena Garcia," Alice introduced her. "She has been assigned to take the lead on the investigation into your case."

"We wanted to come up and give you an update on the case in person, and to see if you'd remembered anything further," Alice continued.

"Thank you," I responded. "I'll tell you everything I can remember."

"Thanks," said Agent Garcia. "The first thing I should tell you is that there won't be a trial. With the mountain of evidence we found, Mr. O'Reagan, at the advice of his counsel, made a full confession. He confessed to more than just the murder of your friends. Apparently, he's done this before. We've linked him to several other missing persons in the area, including one I investigated a few years ago, where we found no evidence of foul play. Your call to Trooper Alice meant that this time he wasn't able to get rid of all the evidence. We found identifiable remains for three of your four friends. Thank you for your quick thinking."

"There will, however, be a sentencing hearing, and we would like it if you could attend," added Alice.

"She will think about it," my dad interjected. "If she is up to it, she will. If not, she won't. I think Beth has been through enough."

I was thankful to my dad for jumping in. I'm not sure what I would have said, but I knew I wasn't ready to face that monster. Maybe in a few months, or years, but not anytime soon.

"Thank you for considering it," Agent Garcia continued. "Your presence there, and words, could help ensure Mr.

O'Reagan never sees the outside world again. If you can't come, though, a written statement or even a video would be helpful. We also want you to know that we have arrested Sheriff Johnson both as an accomplice and for second degree murder. He'd been helping to cover up the disappearances over the years by directing investigations away from O'Reagan and the funeral home, in part by making it appear as though those missing had been lost in the woods. We learned that when they were in high school, Alex's girlfriend broke up with him, they argued about it, and he accidentally killed her. Conor witnessed the whole thing and helped him dispose of her body in his family's crematorium, and he's been holding it over the sheriff's head ever since.

"Lastly, we were able to arrest Conor's wife, Sandra, at a security conference in New York. Apparently, she assisted her husband by setting up all the security systems, locks, cameras, phone jammers, et cetera, so that Conor could do what he pleased. Their agreement was that Conor would only 'practice' when Sandra was out of town, so she wouldn't be directly involved. As far as we can tell, the whole town knew something was up, but everyone was scared of the sheriff and of Conor. No one knew exactly what was happening, and they didn't try to find out. They can all rest easy now, knowing we will be putting the two of them in jail. But they'll also need to live with the guilt of not doing anything to stop the murders."

I couldn't believe what I was hearing. I knew Sheriff Alex was a little off, but that he was complicit blew me away. And to think that that no one did anything about it, and that Conor's wife had even *helped*? I secretly hoped the town would burn.

"Enough with the formalities," Alice brightened up. "Didn't someone say coffee was on? It was a long drive."

Once I had assured them that I was doing well, and we'd had coffee and some squares Mom took from the freezer and warmed in the microwave, Alice and Agent Karena left.

"That was nice of them to drive all the way here," Mom commented. "What a lovely gesture, and so much better than a phone call or email."

I wasn't sure whether I would go for the sentencing or not, but it sure was nice to know I had my folks and the police on my side.

And then there was Michael. Who was he, really? Angel or ghost? And why had he chosen to help me? Why hadn't he helped the others?